"This level of humor is one of the hardest to pull off. Most writers on the Humor shelf don't even try. In *Would Everybody Please Stop?*, Jenny Allen rarely misses."

—Jesse Kornbluth, HeadButler.com

"Like humorist Erma Bombeck, yet for the twenty-first century, Allen has a conversational but dramatic performer's voice that comes through in her essays and is a joy to spend time with as she deals with some of the harsher aspects of life . . . These pieces balance out into a well-rounded set of writings that should please most humor fans; the lives of middle-aged women deserve more focus, and so Allen's rich vein of pathos is a welcome addition. Verdict: Lovers of darkly humorous domestic comedy will enjoy this one . . . Everyone should be able to find something to appreciate."

—Margaret Heller, *Library Journal*

"Really it's too bad that Jenny Allen refuses to drink in any bar with a giant fish tank, never called that raw food restaurant to ask for their insanely good German chocolate cake recipe, and caused the annoying family upstairs to vanish into thin air. Because otherwise Jenny Allen is just plain perfect."   —Stacy Schiff, Pulitzer Prize–winning author of *The Witches*

"I wish I could have written Jenny's book. It's something I identify with. Almost every story has an 'Of course, *me* too' quality. The difference is there's a new laugh. It's a huge, belly, deep-in-the-throat, knowing, tickling laugh that makes it something only Jenny could have written. It's also very, very deep."

—Carly Simon, author of *Boys in the Trees*

JENNY ALLEN

WOULD EVERYBODY PLEASE STOP?

Jenny Allen is a writer and performer. Her articles and essays have appeared in *The New Yorker* and *The New York Times*, among other publications. Her award-winning solo show, *I Got Sick Then I Got Better*, has been seen in venues across the country and in Canada. She lives on Martha's Vineyard, Massachusetts.

ALSO BY JENNY ALLEN

I Got Sick Then I Got Better

The Long Chalkboard and Other Stories

WOULD EVERYBODY PLEASE STOP?

WOULD EVERYBODY PLEASE STOP?

REFLECTIONS ON LIFE AND OTHER BAD IDEAS

JENNY ALLEN

SARAH CRICHTON BOOKS
FARRAR, STRAUS AND GIROUX
NEW YORK

Sarah Crichton Books
Farrar, Straus and Giroux
175 Varick Street, New York 10014

Printed in the United States of America
Published in 2017 by Sarah Crichton Books / Farrar, Straus and Giroux
First paperback edition, 2018

Grateful acknowledgment is made for permission to reprint text
from the Luminous Ground website, courtesy of Paul Baranowski.
A list of the publications in which these essays originally appeared,
in slightly different form, can be found in the Acknowledgments.

The Library of Congress has cataloged the hardcover edition as follows:
Names: Allen, Jenny, author.
Title: Would everybody please stop? : reflections on life and
    other bad ideas / Jenny Allen.
Description: New York, NY : Sarah Crichton Books, 2017.
Identifiers: LCCN 2016052305 | ISBN 9780374118327 (hardback)
Subjects: BISAC: HUMOR / Form / Essays. | LITERARY
    COLLECTIONS / Essays.
Classification: LCC PS3601.L42 A6 2017 | DDC 814/.6—dc23
LC record available at https://lccn.loc.gov/2016052305

Paperback ISBN: 978-0-374-53777-7

Designed by Jonathan D. Lippincott

Our books may be purchased in bulk for promotional, educational,
or business use. Please contact your local bookseller or the Macmillan
Corporate and Premium Sales Department at 1-800-221-7945, extension
5442, or by e-mail at MacmillanSpecialMarkets@macmillan.com.

www.fsgbooks.com
www.twitter.com/fsgbooks • www.facebook.com/fsgbooks

1 3 5 7 9 10 8 6 4 2

For Halley and Julie

Lord?

Please don't let me die in a funny way.

Like being beaten to death with a shoe. Especially not my
own shoe. And, if it absolutely has to be my own shoe,
I'd rather not be wearing it at the time.

—Paul Simms, "A Prayer," *The New Yorker*

CONTENTS

I'm Awake 3

Seconds 10

Ask the Answer Lady 21

Canonize Me 28

Me, Flirting 33

How to Tie-Dye 36

Dream On, You Motherfucking Mother 48

Would Everybody Please Stop? 55

An Affair to Remember 58

When I Meditate 61

My Gathas 65

Swagland 71

Nothing Left to Lose 79

Tawk Thewapy 86

I Can't Get That Penis out of My Mind 92

It's About Time 101

Take My House, Please 106

Faking It 116

Can I Borrow That?   119
My Gratitudes   123
My New Feminist Cop Show   128
Scary Stories for Grown-Ups   132
L.L.Bean and Me   147
Hair Today, Gone Tomorrow   154
I Have to Go Now   164
The Trouble with Nature   172
Speak, Memory   177
Can I Have Your Errands?   182
How to Take Dad to the Doctor   187
What I Saw at the Movies   193
What I've Learned   198
Salt and Pepper   204
Roger Ailes's New, Enlightened Code
   of Sexual Conduct   208
Falling   211
Please Don't Invite Me   218

Acknowledgments   223

WOULD EVERYBODY PLEASE STOP?

I'M AWAKE

I'm up. Are you up? I'm not *up* up, not doing-things up, because I'm supposed to be sleeping. I'm trying to go back to sleep. But I'm awake. Awake awake awake.

That's what Buddha said. Buddha said, "I am awake." Buddha got that idea, that whole concept, from a middle-aged woman, I'm sure.

Not that this sleepless business ends at any time. I think you have to die first.

If you added up all the hours I've been awake, it would come to years by now. Fifty may be the new forty, but it feels like the new eighty.

Thank you, that's a very good idea, but I already took a sleeping pill. I fell asleep right away—it's bliss, that drugged drifting off—but now I'm awake again. That always happens! I fall asleep, boom, and then, four or five hours later, I wake up—like it's my turn on watch, like I've had three cups of coffee. Like I've just had a full night's sleep. But if I act as if I've had a full night's sleep, if I get up and do things, I will be a goner after two o'clock in the afternoon. I will confuse the TV remote with the cordless phone and try to answer it, I will not notice any of my typos—I will type *pubic school* this and *pubic school* that in e-mails to people whose public schools I am looking at for my daughter. I will scramble words as if I have had a small stroke. I will say, "I'd like the Drussian ressing," and then I will have to make one of those dumb Alzheimer's jokes.

I could take another sleeping pill, but I worry about that. I worry about becoming too used to sleeping pills. Sleeping pills always make me think of Judy Garland. Poor Judy.

It's funny about the name Judy, isn't it? No one names anyone Judy anymore—do you ever meet five-year-old Judys?—but half the women I know are named Judy. You would probably be safe when meeting any woman over fifty just to say, "Nice to meet you, Judy." Most of the time you would be right.

I am going to lie here and fall asleep counting all the Judys I know.

Thirteen Judys. Including my ex-husband's ex-wife. Who's very nice, by the way.

I'm still awake.

Some people who knew my ex-husband before I knew him used to call me Judy. "Hi, Judy, how are you?" they'd say, and I never corrected them. Who could blame them when they knew so many Judys? Although I did sort of hope that later they realized they'd called me the wrong name and made note of my graciousness in not saying anything. "I can't believe I called her Judy—and her husband's ex-wife is named Judy. She could have been really unpleasant about that, but she didn't say anything at all. What a fine and self-restrained person she is. I'm going to try and be more like her."

Are all my Judy friends up, like me? Judy in Brooklyn Heights, are you up? Judy on Amsterdam Avenue, Judy in Carroll Gardens, Judy in Morningside Heights, Judy on Riverside Drive? I'm here in my bed imagining I can see all of you outside my window—I probably could see a few of you if you waved at me; one of my bedroom windows looks out on a nice-sized chunk of the city. But I am imagining that I am seeing all of you, like the teacher on *Romper Room* when I was little. She used to hold a big magnifying glass the size of a tennis racquet in front of her face so that it was between her and you, and she would say, "I see Leslie, and Barbara, and Scott, and Bruce, and Judy. And I see Karen, and Peter, and Derek . . ." She must have called my name, because I knew she saw me.

That is how I feel about my friends when I lie awake at night. I see them. I see all the Judys, and I see Jackie and Polly and Ellie, Naomi and Cindy and Cathy and the Deborahs (three!). I see them lying there in their nighties, their faces shiny with moisturizer. Some of us lie alone, some of us lie next to another person who is, enragingly, sleeping like a log. How can these people next to us sleep so profoundly? They snore, they shake their restless-leg-syndrome legs all over their side of the bed, they mutter protests in their dreams—"I didn't say Elmira!" and "It's not yours!" They're making a regular racket, and yet they sleep on.

Sleepless friends, I am thinking about you. Judy on Riverside Drive, are you worrying about your rewrites? Bina, are you thinking about your new twin grandchildren? Are you worried about your daughter getting worn-out taking care of them? Mimi, are you up thinking of whom you haven't had lunch with lately? You're 86 years old. That's 237 in wakeful-woman years. Congratulations for hanging in there.

Sometimes, when I first go to sleep for the night, I fall asleep to the television. And this is a strange thing: No matter what I have fallen asleep watching, when I wake up, what's on is *Girls Gone Wild*. I never turn the channel to *Girls Gone Wild*, let alone turn up the volume, but the volume is ear-splitting. How have I slept for even one minute with the volume so high? Am I going deaf? My goodness, those girls must sleep well, when they finally do sleep. I have to change the channel right away when I wake up to *Girls Gone Wild* because—well, of course because I don't want to watch it, but also because I always think about the girls' mothers, and that upsets me. I worry about their mothers, up in the middle of the night, waking to *Girls Gone Wild* on the television set. "That looks just like Melanie—oh, my God."

Look: *Law & Order* is on. I've seen this episode. Do they run the same ones over and over, or is it just that I have seen every single episode that exists? What a scary thought. Fortunately I never remember what happens after the opening scene when they find the body, so I can watch them all over again.

That was a good one.

I'm still awake.

When did I last sleep well? That sleep when you touched your head to the pillow and slept so soundly you woke up wondering how it could be morning when you hadn't even fallen asleep yet? My children sleep like this sometimes, especially the younger one. "Did I go to sleep yet?" she asks on occasion. I didn't appreciate it when I was young, naturally. "Did you sleep well?" people would ask me in the morning, and I would think, Of course I slept well. Isn't "sleeping poorly" a contradiction in terms?

Friends, are you all still up? It seems inefficient somehow for us all to be awake separately. Wouldn't it be great if we could pool all our separate little tributaries of wakeful energy into one mighty Mississippi, and then harness it—like a WPA project, like the Hoover Dam? We could power something. We could get the other awake women in other cities and light up the entire Eastern Seaboard. And have huge middle-of-the-night parties for all the women who are awake.

I should read. No, reading is too hard for the dead of night. It has too many words in it. Including words I might not know. If I read a word I don't know, I will feel compelled to scrawl it on whatever piece of paper is on my bedside table and then hope I'll be able to read my writing tomorrow. If I am too lazy to write down the word, I will have to decide whether to dog-ear the page—bad reader citizenship!—and I don't want the burden of that choice now, in the middle of the night.

Also, even if I do look up a word tomorrow, I won't remember the definition next week. I keep looking up the same words over and over. *Fungible. Heliotrope.* How many times am I supposed to look up the same words? I used to remember the definitions, but I haven't for years. I still know a lot of words, though. *Cleave* is a funny word because it means "to sunder" and, strangely, it also means "to stick to." *Ouster* is a funny word. *Ouster* sounds like it should mean a person, a person who ousts other people, but it doesn't. It means the act of getting rid of someone, not the person who does the getting rid of. *Temerity* sounds like it means "timid," but it doesn't. It means the opposite, it means "brave"!

Timorous is another word for *timid*, but why not just say timid? Timmy was the name of the boy in *Lassie*, the television show. The theme music for the show was melancholy, shockingly so. It made you yearn, it made you homesick, even as you watched it in the den in your home. When was *Lassie* on? *Bonanza* was on Sunday nights, I think. There were three brothers in *Bonanza*: Adam, Hoss, and Little Joe. My sister was quiet and liked Adam the best. My brother wore clothes from the Husky department and so liked Hoss, who was hefty, the best. I liked Little Joe because I was the youngest and so was Little Joe. Also, I was a scamp, and cute, like Little Joe.

I'm still awake. Only now everything is sort of blending together. It's the time of night when I think I may finally be losing my mind for good. Here's a snatch of the theme song from *Lassie*, but it's blending into the Brownie song, the one about "I've got something in my pocket, that belongs across my face," about a Great Big Brownie Smile. Where's my older daughter's Girl Scout badge sash? Why didn't the younger one ever do Girl Scouts? What's in that pot roast recipe besides a cinnamon stick and horseradish and a can of cranberry sauce? What was my old zip code when I lived on Third Avenue? Why didn't I submit that expense account worth a thousand dollars nine years ago?

Instead of going crazy, maybe I will just lie here and regret things. Let's see, can't I blame the really big mistakes on others? Didn't they fail me, didn't they provoke me, didn't they drive me to it? Didn't they just really strain my patience? Didn't they expect too much of me?

No, face it, you did all those things, all the bad and regrettable things. Now you have to sit with it, as Buddha would say. In your case, of course, lie with it.

Not exactly the path to Slumberland.

Oh, look. The sky is purple now, not black. It's going to be daylight. Dawn! How are you, Dawn? How's it going? As long as you're up, I might as well get up too. We can keep each other company.

SECONDS

I'm afraid there's no way to say this without sounding piti-
ful, so I'm just going to say it.

I used to eat cookies out of opened packages on supermarket shelves. I was a child, but still, it was an odd thing to
do. I'd go to the supermarket with my mother and ditch her
as fast as I could, to hang out in the cookie aisle. In my
adult life, I've rarely seen an opened package of cookies in
a supermarket, so I can't explain why I seemed to see them
all the time as a child, but I did. And when I found an
opened box or torn cellophane wrapping, I would stand in
the aisle and furtively shove the cookies into my mouth, pop
pop pop.

The thrill of finding the packages was like one of those
dreams when you find twenty-dollar bills blowing all over
the sidewalk—only better, at least to a child, because it was
Mallomars and Oreos and gingersnaps and Nilla Wafers.
Pecan Sandies. Vienna Fingers. Whatever they called the

spicy ones shaped like windmills, studded with slivers of almond. Oh, the joy of it.

I told a friend about this the other day. I thought she was going to tell me she'd done it too; I'd always assumed this was one of those childhood pastimes that most children engaged in but didn't bother to mention as adults, like biting their toenails or picking their scabs.

She looked like she was going to cry. "That is so sad," she said.

I had to wonder: Why had I spent my childhood trolling for food in the cookie aisle at Gristedes?

Ah, that's right. My mother didn't feed me.

That's not entirely true. She fed us—my brother, sister, and me; my parents were divorced—but that's about all you could say. My mother was overwhelmed, my mother had been handed some real lemons in life, my mother was doing the best she could. But, boy. We had food, three or four different dinner entrées—fried hamburgers and lima beans, corned beef hash with an egg on top, fried lamb chops, liver and bacon. That was it, that was the repertoire.

And so little of it! I don't remember being offered seconds, although, really, who wanted them anyway? I remember staring at refrigerator shelves, empty except for milk and eggs and celery sticks poking out of a glass of ice cubes and a jar of green olives, there to be made into cream-cheese-and-olive sandwiches for my school lunch, which I hated and which mortified me. Things can't have been this bad; there must have been more food around—I remember now that she liked to make Rice Krispies Treats when the spirit moved her—but honestly, the cupboard was pretty bare.

You never knew when you were getting fed. You weren't allowed to ask, you weren't even welcome in the kitchen half the time. She needed it to herself, the better to curse my absent father and burn things. This was as unpleasant as the sameness and not-enoughness of the food—the tension around it, the joylessness with which it was served.

College food was like a dream. I couldn't believe it: Every day, three times a day (the *same* three times a day!), cheerful ladies in hairnets produced food so delicious it made me want to weep with gratitude. London broil one day, Swedish meatballs the next, barbecued ribs, roast chicken, fish not in a stick. Food cooked with spices! Garlic, tarragon, curry! And that was just lunch. Five hours later, amazingly, they did it again. I couldn't believe the variety—it took weeks before they repeated an item, and you even had a choice of main dishes: fillet of sole *or* Salisbury steak; shepherd's pie *or* macaroni and cheese. And sometimes there would be a theme—Chinese Banquet (water chestnuts! crunchy noodles!), South of the Border, Mangia Italiana. The other kids made fun of Theme Nights, but I thought they were thrilling. I couldn't believe we were being made such a fuss over.

Incredibly, there was dessert every night—Jell-O with little ridged minarets of whipped cream, tapioca pudding and rice pudding and bread pudding and chocolate pudding. Chocolate cake. Chocolate cake! Just on any old Tuesday night! It was like a party every day, a party celebrating us for no reason other than that we existed.

And there were seconds. "Sure, honey, just hand me your plate. You must really like broiled scallops." Yes, I surely do, and may I have a little bit more of that butter sauce on top, please?

And the next morning there would be bacon and French toast, and a choice of scrambled or fried eggs, and bagels and muffins. I never ate the fresh fruit—why fill up space in my stomach that could be better served with six or seven slices of bacon?

It took me about three weeks to gain twenty pounds. I didn't care. I was in heaven.

I am in heaven just writing about it, just remembering it. It's not like I'd never experienced big, tasty meals before I went to college—my father and his new family loved to eat, and I had many delicious meals at their house. But college food, the orgy of it, was the antidote to the food at my mother's house. It just kept coming at you, and you didn't even have to worry about whether you were quick enough to offer to help do the dishes. It was just given to you—well, not given, but it felt that way.

I graduated from college eventually, but that excitement about eating has stayed with me every single day of my adult life. Three times a day—more, if I feel like it—I can choose things I like to eat, and eat them in peace. I never take this freedom for granted, I never get tired of it. I never don't anticipate eating with pleasure.

This is how much I love eating: The first time I ate soft-shell crabs—an experience so sublime that if you have not yet had it, I urge you to as soon as possible—I broke out in hives, head to toe. It is the only time I have ever had an allergic reaction to something I've eaten. The second time I ate soft-shell crabs, I—you know, I think that's all I need to say. That there was a second time, that I tried them again, hoping against hope that the hives had been a freak event, sort of says it all, doesn't it?

You are wondering how fat I am. Let me say this: If I lived in most places in the United States, where the all-you-can-eat restaurant is part of the landscape, I would probably weigh 350 pounds. But until recently I lived in Manhattan, where the ridiculous rents won't allow for "family-style" restaurants, so I'm usually about twenty pounds overweight. At the moment, I weigh 150 pounds. I am tallish—five feet eight—and "big-boned," so I carry it off, more or less. I try to lose five pounds sometimes, and sometimes I do, but then I forget I'm trying to do it and order the tartufo.

I have been heavier than I am now, but I thought I looked okay then too. For a few years, I generally weighed about ten pounds more than I do now, and it was not unusual for me to need a size 16. I'm a little surprised when I look at the pictures of me from that time; I've wondered if I have the opposite of that phenomenon that afflicts anorexic girls, the one where they think they look fat when they are actually skin and bones. I think I look normal when I am on the pudgy side.

And I have been heavier even than that. When I was pregnant with my older daughter, I was hungry all the time, and I used to eat cheeseburgers and drink vanilla milk-shakes for a little midmorning snack. By the time I was eight months pregnant I had gained fifty pounds. I weighed 185. I thought I was allowed; I thought I looked fine. "You think that when you have this baby you're going to lose all the weight," my obstetrician said to me. "But the baby is going to weigh about seven pounds. So after you have it, you'll weigh seven pounds less than you do now."

He was right. I didn't think I looked great after I had my baby, when I did indeed weigh 177 pounds, but I didn't worry about it that much. I just wore my maternity dresses for a few months until I could fit into my old clothes again. Shortly after my daughter was born I was wearing one of the maternity dresses when I went to a reception for a Cuban poet in an elegant Manhattan town house. I sat down on the thick-glass-topped coffee table in the beautifully appointed living room, the better to talk to some poet on the sofa. The thick glass broke, and I fell through the table frame to the floor, where I had to be delicately lifted out (amazingly, unharmed). I thought it was hilarious. It was only after telling this story for a year or two that I realized I'd gone through the coffee table *because I was fat*.

Except for my pregnancy binge, I seem to be able to check myself before I get truly tubby. I interviewed Martha Stewart a few years ago. She doesn't weigh herself, she told me, doesn't "watch" her weight, but she does go on diets.

"When?" I asked.

"All the time."

"Why?"

"So I can zip up my pants."

I have a lot of thoughts about Martha Stewart, most of them quite critical (this is how she diets: she doesn't eat), but I will say that I was with her on the pants thing: that's how I know I need to resist dessert and the restaurant dinner rolls and the urge to polish off the mushroom ravioli that my dinner companion has left on his plate.

And although I say I'd weigh 350 pounds if I lived outside Manhattan, the truth is that even I have outgrown the stuff that's really bad for you. Even I prefer my hot open-faced turkey sandwich sans thick caramel-colored gravy, even I usually turn down sausages with my eggs and french fries with my hamburgers.

But I have a lasting affection for institutional steam-table food—for the food itself, the mashed potatoes and chicken rollatini, and for the sheer heaping plenty of it. I have spent some of the happiest hours of my adult life in cafeterias—employee cafeterias, YMCA cafeterias, the cafeteria at my daughters' public school, where I ate on days I volunteered at the library. I like the cute little milk cartons. I don't mind plastic utensils. I don't mind sporks. I don't even hate most airplane food, and I am actually nostalgic for it when I am handed the seven peanuts in a foil bag they give you now in lieu of a meal. And I am probably the only person you will ever hear say that she enjoyed her meal in the cafeteria at Sing Sing (I went on a tour): sloppy joes, macaroni and cheese, red beans and rice, syrupy canned pears.

I like the one-step-removed quality of institutional eating. I like the cheerful servers, but they don't have to be cheerful. There don't even have to be servers. One of the most memorable food moments I ever had was eating what was billed as a "fresh ham" sandwich thirty years ago in the Horn & Hardart automat on Forty-Second Street and Third Avenue in New York. (For those too young to remember, automats were vast cafeterias that served food from banks of little glass-fronted dispensers, an early version of the vending machine. Behind the dispensers were kitchens, and humans who made the food and replaced it in the dispensers, which sounds depressing but wasn't, at least for the customer.) The fresh ham was thick slices of warm roast pork, and they came inside a big soft roll, and the idea that such a perfect, delectable thing came out of an anonymous window was exciting to me in a way that, now that I am trying to describe it, I realize sounds sort of . . . kinky.

As long as I am going down this road, let me say this about me and food: I like paying for it. I like the cleanness of that exchange. I love restaurants for that reason, but the kind of restaurant I like best is the casual, unfussiest kind, the kind where the waitperson is not interested in introducing himself or telling me he is going to be my server this evening or hovering around asking whether I am finding my entrée satisfactory. I love coffee shops not only because I like the kind of food they serve, but because my server is not that interested in me. There isn't a lot of pressure on our relationship; it's more of a one-meal stand. I like the café car on Amtrak. I like snack bars and coffee wagons and souvlaki stands.

But I also like it free. I don't think I have ever passed up an opportunity for free food. I don't sneak food off store shelves anymore, you'll be relieved to know, but I never turn down food when it's there. Platters of brownies at Curriculum Night at my children's schools, platters of shiny doughnuts in college admissions offices, bakery birthday cake in the office kitchenette, left over from the little party in ad sales. One of the markets where I used to do my food shopping (I don't say *supermarket* here because, annoyingly, we didn't have supermarkets in my New York neighborhood, where the rents I mentioned above had driven them out; we had markets with aisles no wider than a doorway, and dinky carts that looked like children's toys) set out samples of cheeses, sometimes so many varieties it was like running a gauntlet, only a good kind of gauntlet—a cheese gauntlet! I was as happy as I am at a cocktail party, where I also never let a tray of pinkie-sized wienies or spinach-filled papery pastries pass me by without my plucking off one or two or five.

The corollary of always anticipating eating is being nervous about not getting enough to eat. I don't like being separated from food for too long, and I always need to know where my next meal is coming from. My friends John and Goldie gave me a ride from Woods Hole, Massachusetts, to New York not long ago. For the five-hour trip, I brought with me four hard-boiled eggs, two yogurts, a package of baby carrots, and many Fig Newtons, all in a little cooler.

Some of these items had been in my refrigerator, which I had cleaned out that morning. But that wasn't why I had brought my food. I brought it because I had never been on a car ride with John and Goldie, and I didn't know their position on food while traveling. Would they not eat for hours, requiring me to request a bathroom break at one of the infrequent McDonald's on the interstate to get something, anything, to eat, something pallid and microwaved that I would hate?

Goldie and John didn't bring anything; their position on food while traveling, it turned out, was to stop for a civilized lunch. We chose a restaurant off the highway that offered only an enormous buffet, complete with a white-hatted chef carving slices from a bloody roast beef and a pillow-sized ham. John and Goldie looked a little overwhelmed; all this artery-clogging plenty was a bit much. I felt like I'd won the lottery.

If I need to know where my next meal is coming from, I also need to know where my family's next meal is coming from. This can be anxious making (my friend Angeline likes to say that she "forages" in her cupboards when it's dinnertime at her house; my first reaction, when she told me this, was to be astonished that her family still liked her), but mostly it has been a pleasure. I am not a great cook, but I am a good cook. You would like my leg of lamb and roast pork. You would like my spinach risotto, and penne with cauliflower. You would like my pineapple upside-down cake. (You flip it onto a platter when it's done so the slices of pineapple on the bottom end up on top. It's fun to do; it looks like a magic trick and always impresses young children.) I am killing many birds with one stone when I cook—mending that sad old sense of deprivation, and taking care of people I love. It's a win-win for me.

This is how much I love eating: Ever since writing the words *chocolate pudding* in this piece, I have not been able to get chocolate pudding out of my mind—how much I used to love it; how, for some reason, I haven't had any in years. If you get it with whipped cream on top, you can fold the whipped cream into the pudding, which turns it a lovely café-au-lait color and makes it taste even more delicious.

Thinking about it makes me want some right now, but I'm on a train at the moment.

If I didn't have someone meeting me at the end of my trip, and if the next stop on the train was at a town that had a diner within view of my train window, I'd get off the train. I'd walk to the diner, and I would have a big helping of chocolate pudding and whipped cream, hopefully in a tall glass sundae dish. Then I would wait for the next train, and I wouldn't mind waiting one bit.

ASK THE ANSWER LADY

Dear Answer Lady: Before he slammed the door and moved out last month, my husband spent a year looking at me darkly and saying things like "What have you done with the spoons?" Do you think he has a girlfriend?

I do.

Why?

Well, I'd have a girlfriend too if my wife hid the spoons.

They were in the dishwasher!

Answer Lady was only kidding. Seriously, I do think he has a girlfriend. This is the way they get when they are looking to leave.

I think I should google her, don't you, Answer Lady?

You don't even know her name.

Oh, that's right.

Just look at this year's canceled checks from the bank, the checks they xerox so tinily now you need a magnifying glass to read them. See that one he wrote for several hundred dollars to Sherry Waxman, with "research" on the memo line?

He's not researching anything.

Just Sherry!

I don't think it's that funny. This whole thing isn't funny. His patients keep calling me at the house looking for him. He always gives them our home phone so they can reach him in a crisis, and now no one can find him. His office voice-mail box has been full for two weeks, and he doesn't answer anyone's e-mails or cell phone calls. He's a psychoanalyst.

Of course he is. Has he contacted you at all?

He called right after he left, to say that I'd ruined his life for nineteen years. Then he called three hours later to ask for the phone number of our periodontist.

Tell Answer Lady you didn't give it to him.

I almost did, but then I said, "I think you can look that up yourself." And he said, "Oh, I get your game!" and hung up. He did e-mail me once, after I'd e-mailed him the membership dues from his gym. I sent the bill as an attachment. And he e-mailed back, "Please send this to me the regular way. I don't do attachments."

"I don't do attachments"! That's priceless. What did you say?

I think I deleted it.

Very restrained! How good of you not to say, "Why don't you get your girlfriend to do it for you?"

I didn't know about the girlfriend then. The girlfriend! I forgot about her for a minute. Should I google her now?

No, not yet. How's your money situation?

It's awful. It's scary. I have to sell the house, which is

freaking me out, just on a practical level. There's so much stuff here I don't know where to start. And I raised my children here! This is our home!

Take some deep breaths. It helps, really. They're teaching kindergartners to do it now. Okay. You're not going to be that sad about moving, you'll see. You don't really need that big house anymore. Two of the rooms in it are just places where you pile old tax returns and things you couldn't even get rid of at a yard sale, like your broken waffle iron and that old Easy-Bake Oven. Also, your neighborhood has filled up with young couples with toddlers, and the mothers keep bending your ear about their children's lactose intolerance and preschool applications and you're just too old to care that much.

I still like Halloween, though. I like the trick-or-treaters. They're so sweet.

They will have Halloween in your new place, Answer Lady promises. Halloween is the biggest holiday on the planet. Even if you moved to the North Pole, trick-or-treaters would knock on your igloo to take all the Kit Kats and not want the little boxes of Good & Plenty. As far as your own children are concerned, they'll adapt. In any event, they'll be off at college soon and you will be alone in your big house most of the time, racking up those huge heating bills and having to shovel out your driveway when it snows. Move to a nice condo, where they take care of those things.

Oh, my God. College. How am I going to pay for it? And now I keep getting these enormous American Express bills for expensive restaurants, which I now realize are for dinners

my husband is taking Sherry Waxman to. I think I should google her now.

Just hold your horses. About college: Forgive my bluntness, but you two probably couldn't really afford it before this recent turn of events. You'll just have to find a way, like everyone else. I'm sorry about the AmEx bills, though, I really am.

The subject of restaurants reminds me of something. Now that I think about it, my husband may have taken my kids out to lunch with his girlfriend a few weeks ago. He called them on his cell phone to say he was in town and wanted to have lunch. They were so excited because they miss him a lot, but when they came back from the restaurant, they said he brought a former patient he ran into. They didn't like her that much. Apparently she said, "You'd think they'd have a plain old ham sandwich on the menu." Then she took all their leftovers home to feed her parrot. I didn't think about any of this until just now.

Really?

I'm so mad! I can't believe he took my kids out to lunch with her.

You'd be surprised how often this happens, but it's shocking when it happens to you, Answer Lady knows. So now it's time. Let's just go to Google and type in *Sherry Waxman, Idon'tlikeyouville, USA*. Answer Lady is joking about the town.

Don't worry that there will be three million Sherry Waxmans. Most of them are for a child actress also named Sherry Waxman, whose mother is her manager and seems to get Sherry, who has done a national Doritos commercial and is ten years old but Can Play Younger, into the papers every five minutes. Here's the Sherry we want: the Sherry Waxman with a website called madformacaws.com. Are you sitting down?

Yes.

It seems that Sherry has quite a few macaws, as pets, and madformacaws.com is her forum for giving advice to other macaw lovers.

You mean the birds? The big ones with scary beaks?

Yes. Sherry writes that their beaks are often called "can openers" and says they can bite off a finger. But Sherry uses behavioral therapy to teach them how not to bite. She can also stop them from screaming, which apparently they're prone to do for hours on end, and teach them to "do their business" on the toilet.

Good Lord.

She says they are wonderful companions. Her newest macaws are Alexander the Great and Festus. She named Festus after her favorite character in *Gunsmoke*.

So she's older than I am.

She looks that way. She's chunky too. And she has very high poufy purple hair.

I'm surprised my kids didn't mention the hair.

Me too, a little. And she tweets. Most of her tweets are about the cute things Festus and Alexander are doing, but Sherry has other interests as well. Here's one: "YOU GOTTA READ *Siddhartha*—AWESOME! Just read it for the first time!"

My husband would never be with someone who thinks Hermann Hesse is awesome. I liked *Siddhartha*, but he

thought it was a silly book. I think you have the wrong Sherry Waxman.

Here's another: "Sarah Palin BLOWS!"

Well, my husband also thinks Sarah Palin blows, but he would never put it that way, that teenage-y way, and he wouldn't spend time with anyone who does. I'm sure we have the wrong—

And another: "After seven years alone, happily curled up with my honey and watching *Born Yesterday*. Judy Holliday RULES!"

Judy Holliday is my husband's favorite. He loves Judy Holliday.

Maybe this googling wasn't such a good idea.

You said it was okay. You're supposed to know these things.

Everyone makes mistakes. Answer Lady is very sorry.

Do you think he loves her? She sounds like a nut. How could he love her? What did I do to deserve this?

Do you still believe in cause and effect? Don't you know by now that the world is often a crazy and cockamamy thing, a shoddy old fair ride whose drunk operator passed out at the controls long ago with an unfiltered Camel dangling out of his mouth? You didn't know that sometimes the cars come loose and just fly off into space?

I guess I forgot.

And let's be honest. Didn't you kind of feel something coming? Were you two really having a lot of fun before Sherry?

Okay, no.

And about loving Sherry. Maybe he does love Sherry,

Sherry and her shrieking birds, and her blog. This is un-
knowable by you. But you know what? One day you will
think, "Well, even Sherry deserves to be loved."

You're kidding.

Not at all. You'll see. For now, try not to think about it.
Say goodbye to him, and to Sherry.

Just like that?

Just like that.

Goodbye.

That's my girl.

CANONIZE ME

Just when I thought that life might be too irritating to be worth it, it turned out that I have a knack for performing miracles. It's not that hard. It's like practicing mindfulness, like meditating—only, I would say, more directed. More goal oriented. Instead of clearing your mind, you make your mind focus very, very intently on the miracle you want—like making a wish on a birthday-cake candle, only you don't need a candle or a cake. I wished for everything that I don't like to go away, and it did. That is how I became Saint Stephanie, patron saint of the annoyed.

First I caused the family that lives in the apartment upstairs from me to vanish forever. This is because they had twin teenage boys who bounced basketballs on the floor twenty-four hours a day, and because when I complained to their mother last year, she told me, "It's a family building, Stephanie; deal with it."

Then I transmuted the skim milk in the little stainless-steel "cream" pitchers at the Mt. Vesuvius coffee shop in Carroll Gardens into half-and-half.

Then I caused all the little children who have lunch with their mothers at the Mt. Vesuvius coffee shop after Gymborini class to stop shoving french fries into each other's faces and running around the table and screaming at each other and to sit in their chairs and use their "indoor voices."

Emboldened, I tried my hand at smiting things, starting with all reruns of *Two and a Half Men*. I smote them, just like that.

Then I smote those brightly colored French macaroons because they're too expensive and not that delicious. Also because macaroons are supposed to have shredded coconut in them—okay, maybe not in France, but everywhere else—and these are, instead, almond flavored, with no coconut.

I smote the word *muesli* because it sounds too much like *mucus*, and the word *moist* because it's just upsetting somehow. I smote *secretion* because—well, ewwwwww. I smote *helm* when it is used to mean "direct a movie," and *penned* when it is used to mean "write." I smote all of those words that mean "said" but are not *said*: *replied*, *averred*, *demurred*, *retorted*, *remarked*, *quipped*, etc. I smote *chortle* and *chuckle*.

I smote *lover*, because it's gross.

I smote the senseless, offensive capital *R* in *Realtor*.

I smote the phrase *It is what it is*, because I don't get it and no one will explain it to me.

I smote fat-free half-and-half.

I sundered Kathie Lee Gifford and Hoda Kotb and caused them to be plunged each into her own black abyss.

I caused Sean Connery to be thirty-seven again so he could keep being James Bond, as every James Bond who has followed has seemed sort of gay.

I cast Comcast into a lake of eternal fire, and I began with the billing department.

I turned my attention to transportation miracles. You know how when you're driving on an interstate, and the signs at a certain exit say GAS FOOD LODGING, and you take that exit, believing that gas food lodging will be right there, and then there's nothing there, and no signs pointing to the right way to go? And you have to drive around those creepy dark local roads until you finally find gas food lodging in a grubby town twenty-five minutes from the exit?

First I caused signs to appear on the interstates next to those particular exit ramps, and the signs read GAS FOOD LODGING IS NOT NEARBY, BUT IN A GRUBBY TOWN TWENTY-FIVE MINUTES AWAY FROM HERE. DO NOT TAKE THIS EXIT IF YOU HAVE TO BE AT YOUR FINAL DESTINATION IN A TIMELY MANNER. And then I caused signs with directional arrows to appear at the end of the exit ramps, and they said THIS WAY TO THE GRUBBY TOWN WITH THE GAS FOOD LODGING.

Speaking of driving, I smote all "power" windows and doors on cars, as they are the worst invention ever. No one knows why all of the windows automatically seal shut in the locked position sometimes, yet at other times it is possible to open one window but not another, or two windows and yet not the other two; or why all four car doors will suddenly go into lockdown at once, with that scary locking sound—it feels punitive if you're inside the car when this happens, like you're a criminal being transported to jail—but at other times only the driver's door locks, or the two doors in the back. No one knows how to make individual doors (or windows) open or shut except by jabbing, willy-nilly, at the various controls on the driver's-side "control panel," hoping for the best, meanwhile leaving their ninety-two-year-old parents outside the car in the freezing cold, helplessly yanking and yanking at the door handle while their lips turn blue.

I caused the return of car windows that roll up and down with crank handles, and car doors that lock, manually, when you press down with your thumb on that piece of metal that used to stick up out of the top of each door, and I didn't care if it violated child-safety laws.

I transmuted all Porta Potties into real toilets that flushed. In another toilet-related miracle, I cast all single-ply toilet paper into a bottomless pit.

I made flossing bad for you.

I caused the hinges of drugstore reading glasses to not lose their tiny pins after you've barely owned the glasses for a day.

I turned Young Adult Dystopian Fiction into a small animal that was crossing the road, and I ran it over.

On behalf of the math-challenged, I made the metric system go away because converting to feet and inches is too hard, and I banished military time.

I made dreadlocks on white people, ponytails on balding men, man buns, and soul patches go away for unto eternity.

I made it an act of extortion, punishable by imprisonment, for any organization to solicit funds with advertisements showing extremely sick bald children.

In another civic-minded gesture, I created a new federal agency, the Office of Unambiguous Recycling. The only job the agency has is to answer e-mails and phone calls from people who are confused about what does and does not get recycled. People call up and say, "What about those small square plastic 'baskets' that strawberries and blueberries come in? My husband always puts them in the recycling bin, and then I take them out and put them in the regular trash, and then he puts them back in the recycling bin. All we do is fight about it, and I think I hate him now. Who's right?" A live operator gives them a definitive answer.

So those are my miracles so far. Oh, I almost forgot. Remember the family above me that vanished? I caused to move into their apartment an extremely attractive man with an appealing slight Scottish accent. His work, which he is always vague about, keeps him away for weeks on end and seems to require him to wear tuxedos quite a bit. Anyway, he really, really likes me.

ME, FLIRTING

Is this seat taken? Actually, I'd better sit over here, on your other side. My "good ear" side! I'll hear you much better, especially when the band starts up. I should probably get a hearing aid, but I'm saving up for dental implants. I wasn't going to bother because the rotten tooth is way in the back— can you see it, way back there?—but then I thought about the teeth on either side of it collapsing into each other and my mouth caving in, and I decided to just go for it, you know?

Is that a Housatonic? Gin and tonic? Ha! Sometimes the wrong sounds come out of my mouth now. The other day I said "fertilizer," but it came out "dishwasher." Anyway, that looks delicious. I wish I could have one. But carbonated beverages have started to make me so gassy! And brussels sprouts—forget about it!

How do you know the bride and groom? . . . Really? I can't believe they have an investment adviser at their age. My goodness, they look twelve. They must be loaded. Good for them. Maybe they'll loan me some money! Just kidding. You never know, though, right? People our age are always coming down with horrible diseases. You could get colorectal cancer at any moment and need cash ASAP. By the way, you wouldn't happen to know how the whole reverse-mortgage thing works, would you?

Don't look now, but I think that's Seth Rogen, two tables over. Unless it's Scott Rudin. Or Seth Meyers. Or Seth Rudetsky. I don't even know who that is.

Honestly, I don't know any of the celebrities anymore. I don't even care. I still can't believe the Beatles broke up. It just makes me very, very sad.

I'm sorry. I can't help it. I'll stop in a minute. Or not. These crying jags are unpredictable. That's menopause for you. *Menopause* is such a funny word. Because it's not a pause at all, it's more like forever. The crying, hot flashes, you name it, all the really old ladies I know tell me they never end. *Menoeternity*, more like it!

Also, don't you think *menopause* sounds like something you'd buy on late-night TV? "Men-o-pause! Push a button, and the men in your life will stop trying to explain football to you for five whole minutes!" I hope that doesn't hurt your feelings.

Speaking of old ladies, I hope I don't turn into one of those old ladies who's always coughing because she has a piece of peanut stuck in her throat. You know those old ladies? You go out to lunch with them, or to the movies, and they spend the whole time coughing and coughing and driving everyone around them crazy. And when you suggest they drink some water, they refuse. "No, no, *that's* not going to help," they say, as if it's a bad idea. When it's the only idea! It's the only cure!

You know what? I like Yoko now! I never thought that would happen. I like it that she's an old lady and still making art. Isn't it funny how life softens your edges? Or maybe life softens some of your edges but hardens you in other ways. Like, I can list the names of every person I don't want at my funeral. There are people I'd just like to say a final "Fuck you" to, you know?

Isn't it strange? You start out life counting the people you don't want at your birthday party, and you end it counting the ones you don't want at your funeral. Maybe we don't learn anything in between. Maybe we just go through life gathering grudges, and then we die. Oh, God, isn't that so sad?

I'm sorry, here I go again. What a crybaby.

Okay, I'm done!

Look, here comes the salad course. I hope it doesn't have any raw onions in it. Acid reflux alert! Acid reflux alert! It's good I brought a lot of Tums. I love Tums, don't you? I don't know why the person who invented them didn't get a Nobel Prize, I really don't.

No, that's fine. Go check your messages. I'll save your place. I feel we're making a real connection here.

HOW TO TIE-DYE

Back in New York, a raging blizzard has shut down the airports. The lone daily flight to New York out of the tiny airport where you are in West Virginia will not be leaving anytime soon—one or two days, the woman you finally reach at Delta, after hundreds of minutes on hold, tells you.

This was not your plan. Your plan was to attend Parents' Weekend at your child's school, in the pretty rolling foothills of the Appalachians, and go back home, where you could get a cup of coffee that tastes like coffee, not the feeble stuff that people drink here, and buy *The New York Times*.

But Parents' Weekend is over, and here you are, in your room at the Holiday Inn Express. Which is . . . where? Not in a town, exactly. Outside your filmy window is your vista: the interstate, and a sprawl of newish stores—a Walmart, an auto body shop, a ninety-nine-cent store, a store that sells discount cigarettes by the carton and beer by the case, an Applebee's.

The real town, with a Main Street and sidewalks, is several miles down the road, but now it's not a real town, either; Main Street is all antique shops and gift shops and pricey bistros catering to the guests of a grand old resort somewhere near here and to the parents at your child's school. So, actually, the view out your window is more of the real town. More of the real America. It's a shame you don't drink anymore; what a perfect time and place to go on a bender. All your needs would be met—alcohol, ciggies, and a $9.99 steak dinner to wolf down after a happy day of drinking on an empty stomach.

Maybe that temptation is what gives you the idea of doing a crafts project. Or maybe it's that Christmas is coming, and you're thinking about what presents to give your loved ones, if you ever get out of here.

For whatever reason, you decide that making something with your hands would be fun—or, failing fun, something to do. You're not too good at crafts projects—fifteen years after your attempt to make snow globes for Christmas presents, tiny white plastic "flakes" are still embedded in your carpet—but that's what you like about them. You feel like you're seven years old again. Wow, you think, admiring the lumpy little ceramic doodad or limp, worked-over origami bird you've produced, I made this!

Here's your idea: You're going to tie-dye a lot of T-shirts for your young-adult children and nieces and nephews. Tie-dyed T-shirts are very in now, and yours will be made for a song while other, less crafty people will be buying theirs for ninety-eight dollars apiece on Avenue A.

First you go to Walmart, which is right next door to the Holiday Inn Express. Normally you boycott Walmarts because of the company's heinous labor practices, but there aren't yet any Walmarts where you live, so this has mostly been a theoretical position.

You forget all about the horrible labor practices two seconds after entering the store because Walmart is so amazing. So vast, like a store in a dream, endless aisles of shockingly inexpensive things—trinkets, sunglasses, little makeup holders for your purse! Ten pairs of underpants for three dollars!—many of which you toss into a shopping cart the size of a Zamboni that you feel you're driving more than pushing. You spend an hour wandering the aisles in a pleasant fugue state, tossing things into your huge cart.

To your surprise, this Walmart barely has a crafts section. A hunting-gear section, yes, with many Day-Glo orange caps and vests; a candy section, ten or twelve acres' worth: Hershey's bars big enough to club someone over the head with, Raisinets in bags the size of feed sacks, and great buckets of candies you hardly ever see anymore—those pale orange soft ones shaped like big peanuts, white nut-studded nougats. And a hair-care section—also enormous, aisle upon aisle of shampoos and mousses and gels and creams and unguents and shellacs. If aliens came to our planet and Walmart was their first stop, they would say, "This is a species that worships hair, and toothlessness."

The crafts section is so dinky! A few shelves, mostly kiddie stuff—some old *Little Mermaid* paint-by-numbers kits, a few dusty packets of modeling clay. You may have romanticized the people who live around here. You thought craft-making was still going on in this part of the country, quilt-making and afghan-making and such, but everyone here has probably turned to beer and television, like the rest of the world, for their entertainment.

But here, on a bottom shelf, is a tie-dye kit. And here, several miles away in the underwear section, are twelve men's T-shirts for $3.99. Fate is smiling on your project!

You try not to be impatient in the checkout line, where you wait for a long time while the checkout woman and a customer are shooting the breeze as if there were no one on line at all. You gather from the conversation that the customer is going to have a baby shower for her goddaughter, whom the cashier used to babysit. They are practically planning the whole shower right there—discussing recipes for sherbet punch and ideas for the party games. Finally you say, "Excuse me, but I'm in a little bit of a hurry." The cashier and the customer trade a look, and the customer silently takes her shopping cart and marches toward the door. "Everything's not all rush rush rush, you know," she says over her shoulder.

You feel bad. You didn't realize that Walmart is the town square now, that this is where people exchange the news of the day *in a leisurely way*, and that you have ruined their visit. "I'm sorry," you say to the cashier, but it's too late. She jams your purchases into plastic bags, not looking at you.

Back in your room, you lay out the contents of the tie-dye kit on the floor: a big plastic sheet to protect the carpeting from getting stained with dye as you work; a million rubber bands; packets of powdered red, yellow, and blue dyes. You pour the dyes into the little squirt bottles provided, mix them with tap water, and shake them up. You're ready to work!

Not yet. The directions say to wash the T-shirts before dyeing them. You find the laundry room down the hall and exchange several dollar bills for quarters with Rick, the nice day manager. You load the washing machine with the T-shirts, noting that the woman next to you, in a tank top that shows off the array of tattoos on her arms, is doing a surprisingly large load of laundry in the other machine. She explains that she and her husband and kids live just up the street but have decided to spend the weekend here at the hotel as a treat, so she's brought a lot of laundry from home.

While the T-shirts are being washed, you head over to Applebee's for dinner. Teresa, your friendly young waitress, points to your hands and says, "Looks like you've been paintin' somethin'." Your hands, you now notice, have been stained red, the color of boiled lobster claws, by the red dye. You laugh and tell Teresa about your project; she tells you that her fiancé loves to wear tie-dyed shirts and is in a heavy-metal band with Rick's brother, Tracy.

After your T-shirts have been washed and dried to damp as instructed, it's time to decide what patterns you'll make. For the popular sunburst pattern, for example, you pinch the center of the T-shirt between thumb and forefinger and hold up the shirt so that the rest of it falls loosely, like an empty parachute. Then you wrap about a thousand rubber bands tightly around it, leaving a thin section of shirt in between each rubber band. Doing this to twelve shirts takes you five hours. While you do it, you watch a local hunting show on television. The show is simple in concept: Hunters are shown hunting, in real time. In this episode, two hunters crouch behind some bushes, waiting for a deer to appear.

"You think that buck's gonna show up, Steve?" one of the hunters says.

"I hope so, Mike, my boots are sure soaked."

You feel sorry for the buck, but there's something valiant about Steve and Mike, stuck out there in the soggy brush, waiting and waiting. They're like Vladimir and Estragon, only in fluorescent-orange hunting caps.

Now, though it is practically the break of day, you're ready to dye. Carefully at first, and then with increasing abandon, you squirt the different colors of dye onto the shirts, this time not failing to use the plastic gloves provided in the kit. You leave the rubber-banded, dyed shirts on the plastic tarp so the dye can "set" for a few hours.

You wake up in the morning, a little bleary from lack of sleep, but eager to see the results of your labors. You begin rinsing out the T-shirts in the sink, as instructed, to wash out the extra dye. Each shirt takes forty minutes or so to rinse and wring out, and your wrists hurt so much that you wonder if tie-dyeing can give a person carpal tunnel syndrome. By the fifth shirt, you decide to just dump the rest of the shirts in the sink and let them soak while you go downstairs to enjoy the free breakfast buffet, perhaps followed by a soak in the hotel's Jacuzzi.

On the way to the breakfast buffet, you pass the pool room and notice through its picture window that the Jacuzzi is packed with splashing children. Sitting nearby is the mother from the laundry room, who smiles at you and holds up her can of Dr Pepper in greeting.

A chatty older lady named Patty manages the breakfast buffet. She's heard about your tie-dye project from Teresa, she says, whom she used to babysit and who lives next door to her.

"Hon, Teresa told me it looks like you kilt somethin' with your bare hands," Patty says, with a little laugh.

Still a raw-looking red, your hands do kind of look like you killed something. Maybe you'd better go back to your room and give them a really good scrubbing. You share the elevator with the kids from the pool, shivering in their towels. At first they are laughing and pummeling each other playfully, but when you get on the elevator, they look at your hands and fall silent.

"I've been tie-dyeing in my room," you say, a little too brightly.

"Yes, ma'am," a skinny little boy says, and looks at the floor.

You feel like you're lying, or like they think you're lying. Which is so ridiculous!

Back in your bathroom, the water in the sink is a dark, ugly brownish purple. You dredge out the soggy T-shirts and set them on a big white towel and let out the sink water. The empty sink basin is stained the same shade of puce. You

wonder if you'll get a charge on your bill for "sink replacement." Also, the color is upsetting—the color of liver, of
internal organs. It looks like a butcher has been at work in
here. Who could be you, with your red hands and all. But
you've just been tie-dyeing! What are you so worried about?

You buy a packet of powdered bleach from the laundry
room—the mother is in here again, stuffing another giant
load of laundry into the dryer—and, back in your room,
scrub the sink with the bleach, using your toothbrush. The
stain fades, but the basin is still tinged a faint brownish
purple. And your hands—you scrub and scrub them too,
like a surgeon, like Lady Macbeth, but they stay an angry
red. The stain of your deeds. What deeds? It's not like you
murdered someone in here.

But it is, sort of. Someone could think that. And now,
you notice, the towel you've carelessly laid the wet shirts on
is stained that liverish brown. You rinse and rinse the towel
under running water, but still the dye will not wash out.
You will have to hide this towel in your suitcase and take it
home with you. Now you rinse out the shirts, one by one;
amazingly, the shirts have taken on none of the hideous hue
of the sink water but instead retain their bright, separate
colors, each shirt a merry red and blue and yellow. They
look great. They look like festive clown wear.

Working with running water as you are, you don't hear
anyone enter. A young woman is standing there. You scream.

"I'm sorry, ma'am, I thought y'all went out!" It's Briana,
from housekeeping, here with her cleaning cart. Briana is

Patty's second cousin. You know this because Briana is, like Patty, loquacious; yesterday morning, when she came to clean your room, she told you how she is staying with Patty for a while to save on rent so she can pay for her wedding to Ron, whom Ruth introduced her to because Ruth used to teach Sunday school with Ron's mother, and who is Rick, the day manager's, hunting buddy.

But Briana isn't chatting right now—now she is staring at you, and your room, and the bathroom, and smiling in a confused, worried way.

"Oh, I'm sorry! You surprised me. I'm just tie-dyeing," you say. You look at your surroundings. It's awful in here. The purple-brownish sink, for one. For two, the stained towel you rested the wet shirts on. For three, the room is an unholy mess, the mess of a crazed, disturbed person—empty squirt bottles tossed about; rubber bands everywhere; your rumpled, unmade bed; that plastic sheet on the floor covered with dark, pooled-together blobs of dye. There's something sinister about any big plastic sheet. Yours is no exception.

And now you notice a red smear on the wall, from when you steadied yourself with your hand to get up from the floor while you were tie-dyeing.

"Do you think you could come back a little later?" you say to Briana.

"Yes, ma'am," she says, and leaves quickly. Who knows what Briana is thinking. But she's going to bend Patty's ear about the chaos in here, that's for certain. Briana and Patty are probably thinking you have murdered someone, and that "tie-dyeing" was just a cover. Or maybe you're tie-dyeing all of your victim's clothes so that no one will be able to identify them as his or her clothes. Or maybe you're a se-rial killer, and tie-dyeing your victims' clothes is the "art" you create from your kill, your "trophy." What a sick, sick trophy—happy, clownish raiments made from the wardrobe of your kill. Or maybe you slaughtered a school of clowns.

Okay, there's no body. You have that going for you. But there will be, of that you may be sure. Everyone owns a gun here and uses it—even Patty, who is a grandmother many times over, told you she goes hunting every weekend for muskrat with her husband. Someone—some transient, someone like you—will show up dead in a Dumpster in the back of some local parking lot, having been shot in a bar fight or for letting their hound dog wander into someone's yard. Or having been beaten to death with a bucket of nut-studded nougats, for sport, by local hoodlums high on crystal meth.

And you, the stranger in town, will be suspect *número uno*.

You review your alibis. The places you've been in the past hours where people have seen you not murdering someone. The cashier and the customer from the checkout line at Walmart hate you and will say that you seemed *agitated* and *in a rush*. Teresa from Applebee's will note your *red hands* and *suspicious blabbing* about your tie-dyeing project. So will Patty. So will the little kids from the elevator, whose mother—who cannot believe how close her children came to being slaughtered themselves, their little bathing suits turned into tie-dyed souvenirs—will report how she thought it was weird that a single woman was *laundering many men's T-shirts* in the laundry room. And Briana will clinch it, with her description of your *scream*, of the *red smear* on the wall, and of the shocking mess in your room, clearly the result of a *struggle*.

Everyone will think you're guilty because everyone here knows everyone, and already at least five of them know you did it. And they're probably all related to the DA and to the public defender, who is probably the DA's brother, so just forget about a vigorous defense. The public defender will be winking at the jury while you give your lame testimony—"I was just tie-dyeing!"—and his wink will say, *Yeah, right*.

But there's DNA! DNA will save you! Because there won't be any in your room, except for yours—none from your victim! You never appreciated DNA until now. Thank God they discovered it.

But wait, the mother saw you buying bleach in the laundry room. Which anyone who has ever watched a TV crime show knows is what the killer uses to get rid of DNA evidence.

Clearly, there is only one thing to do, and that is to drive your rental car over to the police station and turn yourself in. They won't give you the death penalty if you confess. You'll just spend the rest of your life in the women's prison down the interstate. Your family will visit you, but not that often, because it's so far away. You will pass your days in your cell, being served grits and boiled broccoli on a tin tray shoved through a slot in your cell door.

Maybe it won't be so bad. You've always had a soft spot for grits. Maybe they'll have franks and beans, which you also like, and fresh biscuits. And hip-hop aerobics in the yard. At least you won't have to live like this, in constant fear, which is no kind of life at all, you can already tell.

Maybe there will be crafts projects, as therapy. You'll pass on the tie-dyeing, but you'd enjoy lanyard-making and pot holder–making. That would be fun for you. Or at least a way to pass the time.

Oh, look, here's a text message from Delta. Your flight has been canceled, again. The blizzard back home is over, but now the storm is headed here, and they've closed the airport. All you can do, really, is pray for leniency.

DREAM ON,
YOU MOTHERFUCKING
MOTHER

Something's wrong, here in the backyard. Is something bad about to happen?

Is it the clump of crows, pacing around at the far end of the yard? They take wee, careful steps, lifting their little feet in the air before setting them down, daintily, like ladies trying not to step in something disagreeable. Or, in their aimlessness—each crow has his or her own pointless prancing pattern, oblivious of the others—like dancers in an annoying postmodern performance. But the sound! The sound isn't dainty at all! Like they're being strangled, like they've got pebbles in their throats and are trying to hawk them out. Crow them out. *Ghaghagh! Ghaghagh!* A horrible sound, a sound that should belong to a garbage truck, not a creature of lovely Mother Nature.

A murder of crows, that's what you call a gang of crows like this. It feels very Hitchcock-y here suddenly, very Tippi-Hedren-in-a-phone-booth-y.

Naw, the crows are often here, the creepy things. A

bunch of thugs—just bullies, though, all *ghaghagh* and no bite. They never do anything bad, except exist.

It's something else, something new. Something weirder. What could it be, here on this mild and sunny midafternoon?

Here is your old house, here the hammock slung between two sturdy pines, here the car on the patch of lawn where you always park it, here the big heap of dead leaves you raked seven months ago but have not yet dumped into the patch of woods behind the yard.

The car! The car is here. The car is never here. The car is never here because it is always on the road, being driven by you to take teenagers places—your own teenager, plus various others, for they travel in packs, wearing one another's clothes and changing them constantly so that you are perpetually baffled; Andrea may be Emma and Emma may be Sarah. To Cumberland Farms for Slurpees, to Radio-Shack to replace yet another cell phone charger lost to the universe, out there with all the lost hoop earrings and the stray socks somehow lost though they were part of a clean pair only moments ago.

You are forever driving them to the beach, to the movies, to the thrift shop, to the volunteer job at the horse farm. To the ice cream store. To the drugstore, for twelve-dollar shampoo and for chewing gum. To the friends' houses, where they will feast on nacho cheese Doritos until their fingertips are stained neon orange—you could find them in the dark by their fingertips!—and cut the legs off blue jeans to turn them into shorts so short they would be stoned in some states; to the drugstore, yet again, for conditioner and leave-in conditioner and something also for the hair called serum, which sounds both scary and disgusting; for Nair, and ladies' razors (Nair *and* razors? Another mystery, lost to the universe), and for mascara and mascara remover and more gum. Always more gum.

But now it is different. Your own teenager is not yet in possession of the holy driver's license, but the friends are, and now all you see is the dust behind the wheels of the friends' parents' cars as the children peel out of the driveway at ninety miles an hour, cans of AriZona iced tea the size of fire extinguishers in hand, off on their appointed rounds, for which they do not need you anymore.

They can do their work themselves now—buy the Slurpees and the nacho cheese Doritos, search for the lost lip gloss or stray Teva, left at someone's friend's friend's house or maybe on some bench or other in town. Floating back to you from the car radio, at a volume that would make Helen Keller cringe, come the musical stylings of Nicki Minaj, Kanye, Lil Wayne. And of Mr. Kid Cudi:

Give a fuck about your lifestyle
Give a fuck about a motherfucking lifestyle

Toodle-oo, children! Have safe and yet motherfucking fun out there!

Kid Cudi is appealing, truly. His melodies are so beautiful, and the lyrics so plangent—"Tell me what you know about them night terrors every night"—and his voice is smoky, drowsy, almost postcoitally mellow.

And Kid Cudi is so right, really, so wise, about the whole lifestyle thing. Your lifestyle has been to drive the car. You are so accustomed to driving the car that you have this constant buzzing in your legs, starting in the very soles of your feet, from being welded these many years to the gas pedal. Like the thrumming car is inside you, like you *are* the car.

And now you have no lifestyle. You will have to get a new lifestyle, if you give a motherfucking fuck about it. And you do! Thank you, Kid Cudi, thank you for the admonition!

You could dump the dead leaves in the woods finally. Not that much of a lifestyle, but it's a start. You dump the leaves, but it only takes thirty-seven minutes. It feels virtuous to have done it, though. Maybe this is your new lifestyle, being a handyman, caring for the property so badly neglected during your driving years. You patch the screen in the screen door, superglue the loose linoleum tiles in the bathroom. Really, that's all there is to do around here, all a handyman can do. The other home improvements, those various odds and ends the old house could use—new wiring, new roof, new boiler, new plumbing—require professionals, and funds you do not have in your lifestyle. Nothing wrong with this old place that $200,000 couldn't cure.

It is surely time to pick up some cash to cover these little extras. You could do that now, with all the time you aren't spending driving the motherfucking car. The list of your talents isn't too lengthy, however. You do an excellent imitation of the Lollipop Guild's portion of "Ding Dong! The Witch Is Dead"—you have the Munchkins' quivering voices down pat—but it's not really a living.

Also, you're good at Marco Polo, the water game, particularly in the role of Marco, suggesting you have some talent in echolocation. Maybe you were a bat in a previous life. Hard to monetize this talent either, though.

You could enter an adult spelling bee and win a cash prize. You have always been an excellent speller, almost freakishly good, practically famous for it.

You are forgetting that your spelling talents have diminished in the last few years. Something has happened to your brain. Here's how you spell *cheese* now: *cheeze*. And all the *s*'s and *z*'s are a problem, not just *cheeze*. *Realise? Realize?*

Quick: How do you spell that flowering bush you're looking at, here in the backyard? *Rhododendrun. Rhododendrin. Rhododendron.* Mother*fucker*!

You could invent things. Maybe Kid Cudi would help you finance them. Kid Cudi is a dreamer—"I'm that man on the moon, I'm up up on the moon," he croons in another tune; he pronounces the words "I'm up-pup-pon the moon" so it sounds like a gentle children's song—and he is off drugs now and feeling very purposeful and positive, you read that in a magazine. Kid Cudi could bankroll your dream of manufacturing small paper towels on a roll that would fit niftily in a purse or pocket, so that when you knock over your cup of coffee at a meeting or drop a shrimp ball on the carpet at someone's cocktail party, you could clean it up without having to make an ass of yourself. Or your other dream, this one more ambitious, of a cloud sweeper, for anxious hosts and hostesses of outdoor weddings and other events: essentially a small plane with a snowplow-style shoveler up front, to continually push away pesky rain clouds during the festivities. Kid Cudi might really go for that.

Maybe then Kid Cudi, flush with your newfound friendship, would sing a rap that you have written the words to. He would write the dulcet, irresistible tune and sing it in that smoky voice that would make it sound like he was singing about something naughty:

I found the package of Double Stuf Oreos
You thought you lost
All up under the shit on the floor of your room
Your motherfucking room
Under three wet bathing suits and all the legs of the
      jeans you cut off
And some empty cans of cherry Coke
And a copy of *Cosmo* and some
Gum you chewed
You gotta clean up this crap
So you can lie down on the floor again, which is
      where you study, which you are supposed to be
      doing, for
The SATs, the motherfucking SATs, so nasty and
Yet so necessary

And the song would be a huge hit with the grown-ups and the young people alike, and you could pay to fix up your old house, which should be fixed up because of all the time you will be spending in it, now that you are not driving teenagers around all the time.

Hark! A crunch of gravel, and music from the car radio

even louder than before, so loud the awful crows finally fly away in a panic, pure earsplitting, throbbing vibration—like an instrument of torture, or some new kind of civil defense alert designed to send the neighborhood population fleeing from their homes, hands clapped to their ears, straight into the nearest shelter before the bomb or poison gas hits. The teenagers have returned.

It is time, now, to set aside the afternoon's dreams. To say goodbye, in the soft light of dusk, to Mr. Kid Cudi and your shared dreamy selves. Now is the time for the teenagers' Nairing of the legs and the ripping open of the Doritos bag and the trillionth viewing of *Friday the 13th* and the quest to come, sure as the motherfucking sun will set, for the lost something or other.

WOULD EVERYBODY PLEASE STOP?

Would everybody please stop saying *iteration*? Who started *iteration*? Isn't it just a stuck-up version of "version"?

Meme has also got to go. You can just say *stuff on the Internet*.

Not everything is *surreal*. Some things are merely *strange* or *odd* or some similar adjective. Going to your college reunion and seeing how old everyone looks isn't *surreal*. It's just kind of sad, and a little funny. You know what's not funny anymore? *Ginormous*. It would be great if everyone would stop saying that.

Could we call it quits with *meta*? *High concept* was an okay phrase. I never thought I'd miss it, but now, with *meta* everywhere, I do. Also, no more *gravitas*. It was such a good word, but all the gravitas has gone out of it. Ditto *iconic*.

Could we stop using *disconnect* as a noun? Also *narrative* as a noun? Also *narrative medicine*? No matter how many times people write about it, no one will ever understand what narrative medicine is.

There may be such phenomena as synchronicity and simultaneity—who are we to say?—but not everything is an example of them. When you and I run into each other at Trader Joe's, it is not a wondrous moment of synchronicity. A lot of people go to Trader Joe's, and it would be weirder if I didn't run into you sometimes than if I do.

Vis-à-vis *survivor.* I'm sorry to be a party pooper here, but could we just say *lucky person*? Speaking of party poopers, would everyone please stop saying *spoiler alert* and then giving away the best parts of whatever they're ruining for the rest of us? We haven't seen the movie yet. We don't want to know. Stop spoiling everything.

Unless you are talking about, say, cancer, would everyone please stop referring to the *toxins* in people's bodies? A malignant tumor is a toxin; the bacteria lining your intestines are not. They're supposed to be there.

Similarly, could people please stop calling other people *toxic*? Pol Pot was toxic, but your cranky mailman isn't. He's just annoying.

Could we please stop shortening words and phrases all the time? *My administrative assistant* (or just *assistant*) isn't that many more syllables than *my admin*, and saying *big pharmaceutical companies* doesn't take that much more time than *Big Pharma.* Also, let us bring back *to make a* in front of *long story short* and eliminate *Safe home* in favor of *Get home safely.*

Could we lose *Have a good one* and go back to *Have a good day*? Or, better, *Goodbye*?

Would everybody stop saying *To your point* and, unless you mean the actual end of a particular day, *At the end of the day*? If you had to do a shot every time some expert on NPR said *To your point* or *At the end of the day*, you would be roaring drunk five minutes into *All Things Considered*.

Re: *It's all good*. Let us please, please retire this turn of phrase. Not all of it is good. Some of it is good—fantastic, even—but some of it is tragic. Regarding sad events, let us quit saying *Get over it*. It's too mean. We're trying to get over it.

Also, could we terminate *sweet spot*? It sounds like a sex term, like another word for *G-spot*.

Deplane is a word that the airline industry made up, like *Jetway*, to make airplane travel sound efficient and glamorous. Unless we are flight attendants, we don't have to use that word. But regular people say it all the time now; the plane's wheels touch the runway, and everyone hits their cell phones: "Hi, honey, we're deplaning in about ten minutes." Especially since airplane travel is now grueling and horrible, and we are often deplaned before our flight even takes off, saying *deplane* gives this act a kind of self-importance it doesn't deserve. Better to say, "After we sat on the runway for two fucking hours, they canceled the flight for no fucking reason and we all had to get off the fucking plane."

Thank you so much for cooperating. Goodbye.

AN AFFAIR TO REMEMBER

I was flying on an airplane the other day when my new pen splattered black ink all over the front of my new dress. The pen was my favorite kind of pen—or was, until then: a Bic Z4 Roller. The real ink was what had made me love Z4 Rollers. It was thinner than what came out of, say, a regular Bic pen, which meant you barely had to touch the paper to get the pen to move across it. Z4s were like fountain pens, only without the messy qualities of a fountain pen. I loved them deeply.

I loved my new dress even more, though. It was from Banana Republic, and I paid full price for it, which I never do. But the dress was worth it. It was casual and a little dressy at the same time: sleeveless, with a scooped neckline, a tailored waist, and a slightly puffy skirt. It had flattering thin vertical blue-and-white stripes, and the fabric was a blend of cotton and something man-made that nevertheless felt soft and not fake and yet required no maintenance—no dry cleaning, no ironing. The dress practically sprang itself out of the dryer and stood up on its own, wrinkle-free and ready to go. Also, it had my favorite feature in a dress, which is pockets. They were hidden pockets, sewn into the seam, which I like even better.

On the plane, I attacked the big wet splotches of ink with water and a napkin; if anything, this seemed to set the stains. As soon as we landed, I ran to an airport store and bought one of those little travel packets of disposable cloths soaked in stain remover and tried scrubbing the splotches again. I knew this would be futile, and it was. I went to my hotel, changed my clothes, and put the ruined dress into my suitcase. I couldn't bear to throw it away; maybe someone would invent a magical ink-stain remover in the next week and I'd have thrown out the dress for nothing.

Sometimes, when something bad happens to me, I play a little game. The object is to ask yourself if the bad thing that just happened has any silver lining whatsoever. It's corny, but comforting; if you try it, you'll be surprised. There's some good thing even if it's tiny, even if you have to strain for it, in almost every misfortune. I never thought I'd say it, but I can even see the upside of having had cancer. It took me a long time to feel that way, and I won't get into it here, but if you don't die—a big caveat, I know—there is one, I swear.

But I have thought and thought about my ruined dress and what the upside of it could be, and I just cannot think of one thing.

I put this question to a friend, and she said that the ruined dress was one of those lessons about the impermanence of things, about nonattachment. About how everything changes and how life is about letting go.

I considered this. And then I thought, I already know that. Doesn't everyone over, say, forty know it? Haven't we all lost a lot of things? In fact, not to sound too dreary, but doesn't it sometimes seem as if life is just one big leave-taking after another—to your children, to Checker cabs, to weather that makes sense, to people we love who move far away, or die too young?

So much loss! A new dress isn't a show of attachment to material objects (okay, maybe a little). I knew the dress would start looking shabby one day. Buying a new dress is an act of hope, a show of spirit in the face of an unreliable universe.

At least that's what *my* new dress was. It had been a trying year. And now my emblem of hope had these big black splotches all over it.

But you know what? Here's what I'm attached to: possibility. Pleasure. They're less lofty than hope, less credulous, less faith based, but they're more accessible. I went to the flea market yesterday, and I found a pretty little platter. It's practically ordering me to roast a chicken, invite a couple of people over, and serve the chicken on it. I think I'll make peach cobbler for dessert. Someone, probably me, could drop and break the platter during the evening—it's unlikely, but possible, like the ink exploding from my pen—but was that a reason not to buy it?

Me and my dress—we were great while we lasted. Never mind. That's the way some love affairs go.

WHEN I MEDITATE

When I meditate, I like to think about all the things that are happening right that second that I don't know are happening but will later hurt me. This is known in meditation parlance as staying "in the present," "in the moment," or, because I do it while breathing deeply in and out, which focuses me, "in the breath."

When I do this, I know that I have prepared myself for whatever fiasco is surely making its way to me. I will face the impending misfortune with calm equanimity rather than agitated reactivity or ego-driven self-pity. I will not say, as so many do when the bad thing happens, "Just when I thought things were going so well!" or "What the hell?"

In other words, I expect the unexpected. This state of thoughtful preparedness is known as mindfulness.

As I sit in tranquil repose, I make an orderly mental list of events that are probably transpiring in that moment:

Diseases

- I have an infectious disease. But I don't know it, because it is the kind of infectious disease that is undetectable until moments before you die, in a sudden, violent paroxysm, greenish foam trailing from a corner of your mouth. In my case, this will probably take place in public—say, outside the Dunkin' Donuts on Thirty-Fourth Street, near Penn Station. No one, including my children, will go near my body, which public-health workers in hazmat suits will bury in some potter's field in Queens, my cold hands still clutching my Caramel Apple Croissant Donut.

- Someone is spreading a rumor that I have an infectious disease, even though I don't, and no one will ever ask me over for dinner again.

- I have some other disease, also as yet undetectable. It is not infectious, but eventually my face will be covered in unsightly sores, and there go my dinner invitations.

- I have an undetectable disease that is not infectious but everyone thinks it is, and bye-bye dinner invitations.

Weather

- A squall is brewing right now over the ocean near my home. By the time it arrives at my property, the storm will have grown into a full-blown twister that will lift the roof off my house and deposit a flock of disoriented seagulls and a barge's worth of slimy seaweed onto my head.

Escaping Pets

- The seven llamas down the street from me, kept by my peculiar neighbors as pets, have escaped from their pen and are making their way to my house. They will devour my lawn and terrorize me by spitting at me and biting me with their sharp "fighting teeth." This episode will be written up in the local paper in a lighthearted way, and I will be kidded about it by townspeople for the rest of my life.

Odorless Gases

- Odorless yet toxic gases are presently being released from the polluted ponds in the wetlands that surround me, slowly but surely laying waste to the brain cells of all local residents, resulting in psychosis.

Mistaken Identity

- At this moment, someone at the IRS is preparing an audit of me, only it's an audit of someone who has stolen my identity and is passing herself off as me. IRS agents will show up at my door, dismiss my protests, and arrest me, sending me to prison in Louisiana, where I will be put to work on a chain gang and die of sun poisoning.

As I work my way through my list, of these and so many, many other possibilities, I can feel my body and mind achieving the state of calm abiding that is meditation's greatest gift.

I accept whatever is about to befall me, knowing that bad fortune is, after all, ephemeral. It will pass, as surely as water flows through a riverbed, replaced by some different, probably worse misfortune, such as when the river overflows and floods your basement and destroys your brand-new furnace, which cost $23,000. Serene in my readiness, I add it to my list.

MY GATHAS

Gathas are small verses or poems which we use to help us in our mindfulness practice. Usually we learn them and recite them silently to ourselves whilst we engage in a certain activity . . . A great practice is to use gathas that we find inspiring, and to compose our own gathas to help ourselves and others to develop mindfulness in our daily life.

—Website for Luminous Ground, Buddhist organization

Driving the Car

Getting into my car,
I vow that I will drive with
Mindful care and caution
If in fact this is my vehicle
For I often step into
Someone else's car

By accident
If I have done so now, here in the parking lot of
    Stop & Shop,
May I smile with self-compassion,
And not curse my cluelessness,
For the cars where I live are all Subarus,
And all the same model, and all the same
    "Jasmine Green"
A vast forest of Foresters

Going to the Movies

Taking my seat in the movie theater,
I am excited to be here, and
Offer my heartfelt hope that it is not
A movie like *Carol*,
Beautiful but so boring
I loved the period costumes, but
Wearied of the endless shots of the movie stars gazing
    soulfully
At each other, or
Staring into space
Like mute people
"I love talking to you," one of the women said to the
    other in one scene,
Which was strange, because
They hardly talked at all
May this be a movie with more dialogue,
And fewer close-ups
And way better sex scenes

Using the Phone

Breathing in, I call the operator to report
A suspicious voice mail from a person claiming to
 represent
My credit card company
Then I remember that there are no operators anymore,
 as there is
No "phone company"
Breathing out, I turn this moment of agitation into a
 reflection on how everything changes
And remind myself of other bygone things I used to
 complain about but now sort of miss:
Rockefeller Republicans, airplane meals, Sonny Bono,
 Tom Carvel,
Times Square when it was
Nasty
And men who leered at me on the street
On second thought,
Maybe not Sonny

Washing My Face

Washing my face, I thank my skin for being there,
 for each and every pore of it
What a wonderment it is!
I note the long red scar down my left cheek, the result
 of a recent Mohs surgery
To remove a tiny skin cancer
I note how the scar looks like I have
Slept funny, leaving a crease on my face

Except that this crease seems to be permanent
I tell myself that permanence is an illusion, and that
The scar will disappear with my corporeal self
Meanwhile,
One day, perhaps, I will get used to it,
And not want to weep whenever I see myself
In a mirror

Brushing My Teeth

Brushing my teeth, I consider the
Turkish Taffy, Sugar Daddys, and
Bazooka bubble gum
Of my youth,
And marvel that I have any teeth left at all
Even if they require a lot of time in the dentist's chair
Although the crown covering my new root canal is merely
    temporary,
Because I never went back to get
The real one
I give thanks to my crown for hanging in there

Swiffering

Swiffering my floors, I offer gratitude to the Procter &
    Gamble company
For a marvelous cleaning product, although I know that
There is some thought that P&G stole the idea of
    electrostatic cleaning cloths from a Japanese firm
And that the Swiffer Sweeper is based on the "razors and
    blades" model—that is, I must keep buying expensive
    new replacement cloths endlessly

Nevertheless!

I love its silence, so unlike the infernal noise of the vacuum
cleaner

This silence has changed my life

Allowing me to clean my house,

A chore I do not enjoy,

While talking to my friends on the phone

A win-win for me

Doing the Dishes

Breathing in, I wash the dishes,

Aware of their usefulness in holding

Nourishing meals that have sustained my family for many
years

I wonder why it is always, always me doing the dishes

By myself

And whether, interconnected as all human beings are,

This may be the one exception

Breathing out, I release my feelings into the universe, ever
hopeful that someone somewhere

Will sense my need

And offer to help

I open my heart to the possibility of this miracle

At the Workplace

Today I vow to regard my coworkers serenely, with

Loving-kindness and without judgment

This one, who appears not to bathe and has a pungent odor,

That one, who leads the e-mail clique trash-talking the
rest of us,

Are merely creatures caught in *dukkha*, or suffering
May they one day be made whole and not so messed up
Or at least transferred to another department
As for my boss,
Who fits exactly the description of the people in
The Sociopath Next Door,
I reflect on the fact that "What goes around comes around"
Is most often not true, and that
Karmic comeuppance is rarely meted out in this life
Yet patience is all
May she spend her next life as a
Howler monkey, her screeches heard only by the other
     creatures
In some sweltering rain forest
Far, far away

SWAGLAND

We didn't know. It seems incredible, but we didn't.

We had no idea.

My daughter was in a movie that was having its premiere at the Sundance Film Festival. I was her date, for one reason. When you're in an indie movie that gets into Sundance, this is how much the producers pay for you and a loved one to fly to Utah and stay in a hotel in Park City: zero. So if your mother offers to buy you a plane ticket and pay for a hotel, you accept the offer, even if it means taking her with you.

Before we went, my daughter had gotten an e-mail invitation, through her agent, to a party: come for lunch cooked by a chef, and an afternoon of skiing. She RSVP'd yes, saying she would be bringing a guest. A message came back saying that our arrival time was to be 12:30 p.m., as if it were an appointment. This should have been a tip-off, but what did we know?

Another missed red flag: The party was being held at something the invitation called —— House, only it was the name of a ski jacket company. Maybe it was . . . a store? A house owned by the ski jacket company as a perk for its executives? Like Andy Warhol, we didn't care—we were happy to go, having nothing to do until my daughter's movie that night. And we like lunch; we like skiing.

It pains me to share this, but we dressed warmly, in clothes suitable for winter sport. We wore layers. We brought gloves and hats. We wore thick, sensible socks.

A cab drove us to a mountain. At the bottom of the mountain was a big silly wrought-iron gate and a security guard, who checked us off a list and waved us on. We wended our way up the mountain, high, high up; eventually, our cab pierced through the cloud level to the clear air above, air so thin that breathing it felt like you had just chain-smoked a pack of Marlboros. The landscape belonged to a Dr. Seuss book—from up here, the houses far below looked like tiny Whoville.

Here above the clouds were giant, hulking houses, more conference-center-sized than house-sized. Though built yesterday, in a trice, they were meant to summon the idea of "lodge," of "rusticity," all rough-hewn timber and rock-of-ages stone. The taxi delivered us to one of the houses, where a large man who looked like a bouncer let us in. At the door, a smiling young woman greeted us, checking my daughter's name off a list on the clipboard she carried. Was my daughter still up for skiing? she asked. Great, she would just get her outfitted. She whisked her into a bedroom to try on ski boots. "But my mother—" said my daughter loyally. "We'll do her later," said the young woman. I didn't know why, but I understood that later seemed unlikely. Never mind; I would just wander around.

This was such a strange party. First of all, it lacked guests. Aside from us, there were no guests. Instead of guests, the living room was filled with racks of parkas and puffy ski pants, like a clothes store. Many young women milled around, women who seemed to be here in a working capacity, all of them in very tight jeans, and long blond hair ironed flat as a sheet of glass. The dining room table was covered not with a cloth or buffet plates and forks and knives wrapped in napkins but with clunky cameras and photo equipment. Two photographers sat at the table, quietly eating sandwiches out of paper wrappings.

Clearly, they were not being offered the same food we party guests had been promised in our invitation. So far, our party seemed to be hostless as well as guestless. I worried that it was going to be chefless and lunchless as well.

I found the gleaming state-of-the-art kitchen. Here, sitting at a round table, were four more young women—more ironed hair, more fleeting smiles in my direction, the kind of smile people give when you sit down in an airplane seat next to them: I acknowledge you are sitting down next to me, but this is the end of our relationship; we are not going to make friends. They sat with their laptops in front of them, having a meeting of some kind. Not very partyish of them, I thought.

Here, standing at attention by the stove, were not one but two chefs, a young man and a young woman. They would be delighted to make my lunch, they said, and showed me an elegant sample lunch on a plate—pistachio-crusted sea bass, slivers of vegetables inside a little shredded-potato basket. Yes, please, I told them, but first I'll see how my daughter is doing.

Here she was in the living room, cocooned inside a stylish chocolate-brown down parka and black ski pants, new knit ski cap on her head, new ski gloves in her hand. "So I'll return these when I'm done skiing?" she was saying to the young woman with the clipboard.

"No, no," said the young woman. "Keep them."

Keep them? Really? We looked at each other. What kind of party was this? At that moment and not before—amazing, I know, but it's true—we realized it: This wasn't a party at all.

"Mom," my daughter said under her breath, "This is all *swag.*"

We weren't total naïfs. We knew what swag was: free stuff that companies give you to promote their products. We'd even seen what Sundance swag looked like. Our family had been to the film festival a year earlier, when my daughter had a part in another movie shown there. At the Salt Lake City airport on our way home, we ran into a longtime movie star we knew a little. Usually withdrawn to the point of sullenness, he was beaming. "Check these out!" he said, lifting a jeans leg to show off his swag Frye boots. "And this!" he said, waving a brand-new cell phone in the air. "I had to buy suitcases at Target to get everything home!" And all he'd had to do, he said, was have his picture taken with his new purchases.

Later, I had given my daughter an earful on the subject of wretched excess and the way Some People sell their souls cheap.

She listened. She knows that growing up on the Upper West Side of Manhattan means always having to feel you're guilty. That's a joke, but not really. Your parents may send you to private school, but they send you to public school first, so you'll always know how lucky you are. They don't send you to summer camp without reminding you of all the poor children who can't go. They spend half the holiday season shipping off presents to needy children they never met and who aren't you.

We should have guessed that we were in a swag den, but we didn't. We didn't know how swag was delivered. In real life, this house was owned by some nameless rich people; during the festival, when the ski jacket company rented it, it became a swag house. Swagililand. Swagadoon.

One of the photographers was taking my daughter's picture in her new clothes: click, click, click, click, click. The young woman with the clipboard led her downstairs, where the family room had been turned into another clothes store, only this one sponsored by a famous blue jeans company. And now she was outfitted in a jean jacket and form-fitting jeans. Three young women hovered around her like handmaidens, fetching different cuts and styles of jeans, complimenting her contours, pressing her to take one of every kind. Or like Cinderella's fairy godmother, magically dressing her in her beautiful ball attire, only at this ball everyone would be attired in blue jeans.

·

I could see the confusion in my daughter's eyes. She'd been raised to feel guilty, but she was also a twenty-one-year-old with free clothes literally being thrown at her. It was time, if for perhaps the first moment in my life, to keep my mouth shut.

"I know it's terrible to say," she said, "but I love it."

A cheerful young woman, a professional skier, arrived to take her skiing. The skier had been hired to ski with her and give her a free lesson in her new outfit. I was going to be beyond a third wheel; I was going to ruin the photo op. That was fine: I was hungry, and it had started to snow outside. Off they went, a cameraman and a photographer in tow.

Two or three young actors appeared over the next hour or so. I recognized one of them, an actor I'd seen in small roles in films, but I couldn't remember which films. The actors and their retinues left minutes after they came; like trick-or-treaters, they arrived in the foyer looking both anticipatory and dying to go, staying only long enough to collect their gifts and have their pictures taken before fleeing, off to stalk more swag.

The chefs cooked me lunch. I was the only one for whom they cooked lunch, all the other visitors having declined the offer. I ate it while chatting with the chefs, standing at the kitchen counter, the kitchen and dining room tables being unavailable and the living room being a store. The young women at the kitchen table, all from the marketing department of the ski jacket company, typed into their laptops. Other young women—some from the ski jacket company, some from the blue jeans company, one from a sneaker company whose sneakers were on display in yet another room—sat around in various rooms, bored, or watched the snow fall outside the enormous picture windows, or talked on their cell phones.

I picked up a nylon sports wallet from a display arranged on the living room hearth. I thought, I wouldn't feel greedy if someone offered me this little wallet. I think I could accept it. A girl on duty in the living room smiled at me. Clearly, she was not going to offer me the wallet. The swag was for the Talent. It occurred to me that I could be a terminally ill child, my little head bald from chemotherapy, and she would smile at me in just this way, this you're-not-getting-any-swag way. The photographers, I sensed, felt sorry for me, stuck here as I was, and spoke to me with kind condescension. "Hi, Mom, how's it goin'? You doin' all right?"

Time passed. I talked to the bouncer about his recent foot operation. I declined a martini offered by the bartender, who was promoting a new brand of vodka. I looked out the window at the other jumbo houses and noted how much they looked like the photographs on the covers of *Architectural Digest*, which used to occasionally assign me to write about the homes of the rich and famous. I wondered what I would say about one of these houses if I had to write about it, and I scared myself by pretending that I had to write about this house and all the lies I would have to tell. I would have to say the word *grand*, and I would also have to say the word *cozy*. I would have to say the house was both grand and yet, at one and the same time, cozy. I imagined that there was a penal colony for lying writers, and that I would have to go there, perhaps living in the cell next to James Frey, perhaps sharing a bunk with Lillian Hellman.

Because the house was not grand—or only in the sense that a Disney World hotel is grand—nor was it homey, its interiors absent of any personal effects: no family photographs, no books, no magazines, nothing on any surface. The porcelain vase collection behind glass in the dining room cupboard had clearly been bought by a decorator with a wave of a checkbook; every piece of furniture was spanking new, like a furniture-showroom display. "I just wish we could have gotten the fireplace to work," said the young woman in charge of the blue jeans room, looking genuinely disappointed. One glance at the antiseptically clean fireplace told you it had never been used. Something about all this cleanness and newness felt sinister, as if the owners had been murdered here and a real estate agent had covered up the bloody mess with fresh wall-to-wall carpeting and these stagey trappings.

My daughter returned, her cheeks flushed. She had loved her ski lesson, and she had met Stewart Copeland, the former drummer for the Police, in a gondola! One of the blond young women offered her a cup of coffee. Yes, thank you, she would love a cup of coffee.

The young woman pushed a button on an elaborate, shiny machine on the kitchen counter; steaming coffee poured forth into a mug.

"That's a beautiful coffeemaker," said my daughter.

"We'll send you one," said the young woman.

"Thank you, that's great," said my daughter, polite but calm, now wise to the ways of swag. "I'll give you my shipping address." I eyed the enormous, brand-new eight-burner stove and wondered how to get her to admire it out loud.

NOTHING LEFT TO LOSE

Flip-flops, we hardly knew ye! You were so cute, with those wee appliqué rosettes all along your tops, and so new. And kind of pricey, for flip-flops, like thirty dollars. But now you are gone, because I left you somewhere—under someone's dinner table, or under the backseat of someone's car, or at the beach.

It hurts to think of you smothered in snow now, or bobbing in frigid black waves in the middle of the ocean. What a disservice to both of us. It pains me, and leaves me with so many questions, starting with, how did I get home with no shoes on?

Umbrellas and beach towels, earbuds and cell phone chargers and tubes of toothpaste—everyone leaves these things places. One of the charming things about life is how certain items become a kind of communal property, less owned than permanently passed around. I'm the Johnny Appleseed of drugstore reading glasses, but so is everyone else.

Thanks to others' absentmindedness, I have more brands of shampoo and conditioner in my shower than a CVS, and I don't think I've ever actually had to buy an umbrella. There are always plenty at my house, and not just those crummy ones you buy from the guys on the street during a downpour and that flip inside out with the first puff of wind. Serious ones, with polished wooden handles and canopies sturdy enough to withstand a tornado. The umbrellas change constantly, but my stash stays magically replenished—I leave one somewhere, and another shows up.

I'm partial to the pair of hand-carved African wooden salad spoons someone left at my house after he or she brought, presumably, salad to dinner a few years ago. I figure that if whoever left them isn't okay with my keeping them, he or she would have traced them to me by now and taken them back.

"Oh, crap, I left those salad servers at Jenny's," some wife probably said to some husband. "Now I'll have to call her and go over there and get them. And I really don't have time for her to talk my ear off today."

"So forget it. They weren't even ours anyway. My sister says they're hers."

"That's great! One less thing for me to do. Your sister thinks everything is hers, by the way."

(I have to say here that Tupperware seems to be the one exception to this rule. Have you noticed how ferocious people are about their Tupperware? "And I want this Tupperware back," they say darkly, handing you the guacamole they brought for the picnic. Like your picnic idea was just a ruse to get your hands on their plastic food containers.)

In terms of leaving things places, though, I feel like I'm in another, more troubling, league. Teenaged mothers and their druggy boyfriends hang on to those collapsible baby strollers longer than I used to. Mine were left behind, carelessly, in the trunks of many taxis. There are cabdrivers' children all over New York, I hope, who were happily wheeled around in those strollers for years.

Perfectly good sweaters and jackets and coats of mine are strewn up and down the Eastern Seaboard—left on the backs of chairs in libraries, on the hooks of bathroom doors in hotels, on those above-the-seat luggage racks on Amtrak. Recently, I left a coat at my friend Lynne's house, and when I tried to go back the next day to get it, I couldn't, because I'd left my car at her house too. Someone else had given me a ride home. I'd forgotten.

I was going to brag here that I have never left the tools of my trade—my reporter's notebook with the scribbled notes of an interview, the legal pads I write on, my laptop—anywhere and tell you how I keep them in whatever tote bag I'm passing off as a purse at the moment, and how I keep that purse attached to my shoulder at all times when I travel, so terrified am I of leaving it somewhere. Which is true. Then I remembered that I left a laptop on the ferry from Woods Hole to Martha's Vineyard once. Thank you, whoever you are, for bringing it to the Steamship Authority's lost and found!

Sometimes I preemptively leave things—that is, before

they're even in my hands. Here is how I buy the newspaper at a newsstand: I pay for it and walk away. If it's my local newsstand, where the guy knows me, I can go back later and claim it, but if it's not, I don't. I've tried; I sound like I'm scamming the newsstand guy, and even I don't believe me.

Years ago, I bought eighty dollars' worth of live lobster at a fish store on Martha's Vineyard. I put the bag on top of the car while I opened the car door, and then I left the bag on top of the car and drove away. Minutes later, I heard something slide off my car and checked my rearview mirror: There was the bag of lobster, by the side of the road. By the time I'd turned around and returned to the spot, the bag was gone, snatched up by some enterprising person. I deserved it.

I know what you're thinking: This woman must be drunk all the time. That would be the obvious answer, and if it were true, at least I'd have the comfort of knowing I was wasted when I did these things. But I had to give up drinking some years ago. This is me, high functioning! Truly, I shudder to think of the state I'd be in if I still drank. Shoeless, coatless, probably clothesless, lurching around in an old blanket. If this trend continues, I'll be like one of those Buddhist mendicants, wandering the world with just my robes and an alms bowl. Except I'll probably leave the alms bowl somewhere.

Theories about why I leave everything everywhere:

1. I subconsciously want to return to the place where I left the item.

I like the psychoanalytic ring of this, but I never want to go back to the Hauppauge Holiday Inn Express on I-495 on Long Island, where I left the power cord for my computer last summer—once was enough, I swear. I never, ever want to return anywhere on Long Island after I'm forced to go there for some reason—the less time I spend there, I find, the happier I am—and I never miss the subway car where I've left a bag of groceries or the birthday present I'm bringing to a party.

2. I feel guilty about owning things while others do without.

I don't think so. I don't own that many things, at least not compared to other people I know. My parents had a kind of prewar thriftiness; they may have sent their children to fancy colleges, but they never threw out a rubber band. I grew up thinking that owning three pairs of shoes at one time (sneakers, regular shoes, "party" shoes) was my lucky lot in life, and I've never really shaken that off.

For example, my friend Deborah came to stay with me for a week last summer. Her last night, on our way out to dinner, I asked her if I looked all right. "Um, do you have another skirt?" she said. Apparently, I'd worn the same one every day of her visit. And when friends tell me they've bought, say, a sweater in two different colors because they like it so much, I'm always a little shocked, and secretly worry that they have a shopping "problem."

3. I have other, more important things on my mind.

I can't tell you how much I wish this were true, but I'm usually thinking about what's in the refrigerator for lunch, or whether the mean lady clerk at my post office has a diagnosable mood disorder or just doesn't like me.

4. I have ADD.

Ah, a diagnosis! That would be great. It sounds so much better than "scatty." But everyone has ADD. If you don't think you do, just google it. You do, you'll see.

5. I'm not that bright.

Yes, well, this one has the ring of truth. I help out at a weekly drama class for intellectually challenged adults, and I swear, every participant is sharper than me. In one of the "observation" games we play, we close our eyes and try to remember what the other people in the group are wearing.

"Let's see," they'll say, "Janet has on a plaid Eddie Bauer shirt, jeans with a black cowboy belt, and navy-blue running shoes with white trim and Velcro straps, and Brad is wearing a dark green BLACK DOG T-shirt with a tiny hole on the shoulder and khaki pants with cuffs, and Top-Siders. And striped socks."

When my turn comes, I say, "Dave has on . . . uh . . . boots?"

And at the end of class, they hand me the cell phone and sweater I've left on a chair.

•

Never mind, I guess. I do the best I can, and sometimes a miracle happens. Not long ago, I was browsing at the Dumptique, the big shed at our local dump where people leave their used clothes and books and other people take them for free, and I found a lovely plaid Egyptian-cotton button-down Perry Ellis shirt. I was so happy—it was a perfect replacement for the similar plaid button-down Perry Ellis shirt I'd given up for lost years earlier. Then I noticed that the shirt had three letters printed inside the collar, the way Chinese laundries print your name, and that the letters were the same as the first three letters of my last name, and—well, you know the rest.

And last year, on my way from a commuter train to a fund-raising dinner on Long Island (so much for staying away from there), I changed from my everyday shoes into high heels in the suburban cab, and then I left the shoes in the cab. My friend Polly, who was also going to the dinner, took the same cab an hour later and found the shoes on its floor.

"That's amazing!" I said as she held them out to me. "How did you know these were mine?"

"You're kidding, right?" she said.

TAWK THEWAPY

The following interview with Mr. Elmer Fudd, patient #56778, was conducted by Dr. Marvin Seligman, senior staff psychiatrist at Acme Psychiatric Hospital.

Patient Fudd was found wandering in a forest, disoriented and in a state of mental and physical exhaustion. He carried a shotgun whose barrel had been tied into a large bow, like that on top of a gift. He said that a "cwazy wabbit" had done this, and that this act was the "wast stwaw." The troop of Boy Scouts who discovered the sportsman brought him to Acme, where he was admitted earlier today.

Mr. Fudd told the admitting nurse that he was uncertain how many days he had been in the woods, though he said he is accustomed to spending the entirety of hunting season there.

Mr. Fudd is middle-aged, short, bald, and somewhat overweight, with a disproportionately large head. He pre-

sented as generally despondent and morose, though sudden
bursts of rage and "thin-skinned" hypersensitivity suggest
underlying mood lability. Below are the transcribed notes
of his entrance interview.

Dr.: Why don't you tell me a bit about yourself, Mr. Fudd.

EF: I'm a huntuh. I hunt wabbits. One wabbit.

Dr.: Do you enjoy your work?

EF: Not weawwy.

Dr.: And why is that, do you think?

EF: Because the wabbit always outwits me.

Dr.: "Outrits" you?

EF: Oh, you awe howwible! You'we a meanie! I got a
gun, you know! It may be tied into a bow, but I could still
smack you wight on the head with it!

Dr.: Forgive me, I just wasn't sure—never mind. He
outwits you. Please continue.

EF: He's a twickster. Vewy cwever, vewy devious. Sometimes, when I have my gun wight in his face, he just takes
out a big cawwot and chews on it, as welaxed and noncha-
want as you pwease. This gets me all distwacted, and I
forget that I'm supposed to be hunting him—especiawwy
when he asks me if I've seen any wabbits awound, and if he
can help me hunt for them. Sometimes he fools me by dwess-
ing up as a ballewina or Mae West and kissing me on the
wips, which I hate. Then he sticks his stupid cawwot wight
into the end of my gun, and when I pull the twigguh, all the
buckshot expwodes in my face. And he just waughs and
waughs.

Dr.: May I ask how long you have been hunting this
particular rabbit?

EF: Evuh since I can wemembuh. My whole wife.

Dr.: And yet you continue to pursue him.

EF: My motto is, "If at fuwst you don't succeed, twy, twy again."

Dr.: Mr. Fudd, do the words "perseverating" and "perseverance" have any significance for you?

EF: They both have two *awes* I can't pwonounce?

Dr.: True, but I'm thinking about the meanings of the words. In perseverating, we practice a kind of repetition compulsion, an obsessive need to repeat, over and over, an action that is futile, while in persevering we attempt to attain a realistic and healthy goal. I must say to you, difficult as it may be to hear, that I feel it is extremely unlikely you will ever catch this rabbit.

EF: Who asked you, anyway, Mistuh Smawtypants?

Dr.: But perhaps—just perhaps—you don't want to catch him. Perhaps you have picked a rabbit who is uncatchable, at least by you.

EF: That's cwazy! Why would anyone do that?

Dr.: Perhaps that is what you have come here to Acme to work through. Let me ask you this: How do you think you'd feel if you did catch this rabbit?

EF: Oh, many times I think I have caught him, and he seems to be dying in my awms. He says, "I can't see, evewything's tuwning bwack, bwack . . ."

Dr.: And how does that feel?

EF: Twuthfuwwy? Tewwible. These feewings of gweat shame wush over me, and I say, "I killed a poouh wittle gway fuzzy wabbit!" And then I cwy and cwy.

Dr.: In other words, as soon as you think you have slain your adversary—the very goal you have been struggling so mightily to achieve—you are overwhelmed with feelings of remorse.

EF: Pwetty much.

Dr.: Why is that, do you think?

EF: How should I know! But I always get mad wight away again, because he jumps up and calls me a big dope or turns his wong ears into pwopewwuhs and fwies away.

Dr.: And the whole cycle begins anew.

EF: What the heck am I supposed to do? Take up another wine of wuhk? At this wate stage?

Dr.: Change can certainly be a scary prospect, Mr. Fudd. But what I'm hearing is that you don't even enjoy the successful outcome of your hunt, as ephemeral as it may be. Perhaps being a hunter isn't really who you are. Wouldn't it be nice to explore what a more authentic, happier self might be for you?

EF: No! I don't want to be fixed! I don't want to be cuewed! I'll woose what makes me special! My edge. My dwive. My Elmuh Fuddness. I'll be just another schmuck with a speech impediment.

Dr.: Not at all. You will still be Elmer Fudd. But you will be a much less miserable Elmer Fudd. A more fully dimensional Elmer Fudd.

EF: Where's the adwenawine wush? Where's the dwama?

Dr.: Well, those intense but fleeting feelings, those "highs" and "lows," would be replaced by the deeper, more fulfilling pleasures of marriage and family, of connection and community and love.

EF: Will I have to go to PTA meetings? Will I have to assemble compwicated toys at midnight on Chwistmas Eve from instwuctions that have been twanslated into mangled Engwish fwom Japanese?

Dr.: Probably.

EF: Will I have to pwetend to be intewested when my wife talks about pwobiotics? Will she have a bunch of weh-watives whose names I can nevuh wemembuh? Will I have to say "Stop kicking my chaiw" to my childwen at the dinnuh table for eighteen yeaws? Will I have to go shopping at Macy's on Bwack Fwiday with the west of humanity?

Dr.: Well, all those things are a part of ordinary life.

EF: Can I say something?

Dr.: Of course.

EF: Yecch! It sounds excwuciating!

Dr.: Do you mean boring?

EF: To say the weast!

Dr.: It's not as boring as you think. There are moments of great excitement, great stimulation.

EF: What moments?

Dr.: Well, there's sex, for one thing.

EF: I don't even know what that is.

Dr.: Then you're in for a treat, Mr. Fudd.

EF: Is it wike hunting that cwazy wabbit?

Dr.: I'm sorry, I'm not following you.

EF: Is it humiwiating and fwustwating, and aftewud do you feel the pain of wegwet?

Dr.: No, not usually. Only sometimes.

EF: Weawwy?

Dr.: Yes.

EF: That's good enough for me. I'm in.

Mr. Fudd seemed greatly cheered by this prospect, break-ing into sudden staccato laughter ("Huh uh uh uh uh uh uh!"). At this moment, this interviewer experienced a sudden sinking realization: Mr. Fudd is hardwired to experience pain as pleasure. It is his nature, nothing less.

Perhaps, earlier in his career, this interviewer would have recommended to Mr. Fudd an extended course of psycho-therapy. But experience has shown that for patients such as Mr. Fudd, all the talk therapy in the world will not alter their behavior. Electroconvulsive and/or cognitive behavioral therapy may effect some change, but it will be temporary. The patient will eventually return to his essential, despondent self.

It is recommended that a bed at Acme be reserved an-nually for Mr. Fudd, so that he may spend several days recovering from the rigors of the useless pursuit of his foe. He should then be released—back to the forest, back to the rabbit who torments him so successfully. Some things you just can't fix.

I CAN'T GET THAT PENIS OUT OF MY MIND

The technology described below has changed considerably since this piece was written—the idea of teenagers e-mailing each other, for example, now belongs to another, pre-texting era, as outmoded as the rotary phone. But parental anxiety about content, however it's transmitted, remains perennial.

—J.A.

The children are sending out pictures of their penises over the computer. Enterprising youth!

I'll be blunt: The penis that came into our house this way was at full attention. Is this funny? I don't know. I really don't know what to think. I'm kind of beside myself.

I sit down at my thirteen-year-old daughter's computer one afternoon. I need to use her computer because my own computer has just lost its "logic board," which means it keeps turning itself off. I don't have the seven hours to spend at the computer store to find out whether the patient is going to live or die. (Who am I kidding? Of course it's dying.)

And here on my daughter's computer screen is her e-mail in-box. I hardly ever see her e-mail in-box except fleetingly, as I pass through the little nook in the hallway where I've moved her computer from her bedroom. Our school, and the entire parenting industry, tells you to have the computer not in the child's room but in a more public, "well-trafficked" zone, so that the child isn't seduced into dirty websites where strangers might try to send them pictures of, oh, say, their genitalia. If I happen to glance at her e-mail in-box, if I happen to even cast my eyes to that side of the little nook, my child scolds me, "You're invading my privacy!" Which I am.

But apparently she forgot to log out this morning. It's such a novelty to be alone with her e-mail. I've never done this before, I swear, but today I cannot help myself: I scroll through her in-box. I don't open the e-mails, but if you have Gmail, which is what we have, the first line of the e-mail appears next to the sender's e-mail name, like a teaser. So I am sort of reading her e-mails, at least the first lines of them.

All of the e-mails are from her friends, I can tell by their e-mail addresses. I'm hugely tempted to read them, but I don't—even though they tell us at school parenting meetings and in parenting columns in magazines and in the parenting segments on the morning TV news shows that looking at your child's e-mail is a parent's right, even a duty. Just the other day, on the *Today* show, I heard a parenting expert exhort parents to read their children's e-mail, and not in secret. Your children, he said, should be writing nothing that you can't read "while standing over their shoulders." Has this man ever met a teenager? Doesn't he know how much they hate being watched doing anything, including eating an English muffin or waiting for an elevator? That even the squeakiest-clean teenagers in the land are allergic to having an adult standing over their shoulders? I'm sure that Mormon teenagers, when e-mailing their pals—*See u in Temple Square! I am sooooo psyched 4 Tabernacle Choir!!!!*—slap their hands over their computer screens when their parents pass by, protesting, "Mother! Dad! This is so my own personal business!"

Apparently civil liberties do not apply vis-à-vis our children and the computer, but I have mixed feelings about spying on children. In any case, these computer recreations were already out of the gate, galloping away with my daughter, long before I learned what they were; I was too late to make any privacy policies about them even if I'd wanted to. By the time I started hearing about them, she already had many secret passwords, and an entire hidden, soundless world of friends, and friends of friends, and friends of friends of friends. I felt like I had hundreds of teenagers in my house, and none of them were ever going to leave.

So this afternoon I read the opening lines of her e-mails, because they are right there for me to see and I just cannot resist. They seem innocuous enough, if sort of schizophrenic— sometimes the children write childishly ("I am so xcited for

Dunkin' D's!!!"), and sometimes they write like gang members, sort of: "Yo, bitch, dat sucks u have yr math tutor now").

But here is an e-mail from someone whose e-mail address has no letters, only numbers, many numbers. And there's no subject in the subject line. The numbers seem so technical, junk-mailish, that I think the e-mail couldn't have anything personal in it and therefore it is all right for me to read. It's like opening something addressed to "Occupant." Or maybe it's something mercenary, something that is going to cost me money. Maybe she's ordered something from some online catalog, and I'm going to be charged for it every month on my cable bill.

I open the e-mail.

It's a photograph. It's been taken at a weird angle, and it's out of focus. But not so blurry you can't see it's been taken in a bathroom—you can see floor tiles, and a used towel lying on them in a lump, and two large-cupped bras hanging from a hook on the back of a closed door.

And not so blurry that you can't see the star of the picture, right there in the foreground.

Some kid sent this picture. Somebody my daughter probably knows. Oh, my God, are we about to be a statistic? Will someone from *Newsweek* be calling our house in the near future looking for a quote on Babies Having Babies? My baby! My baby who is still young enough to get the child's fare on Amtrak, who likes strawberry milk, and horses, and making brownies? What is going on here?

I decide to print out the picture. I don't know why. Just

as I do it, my older daughter and her friend Desiree stop by for a visit. They're twenty-three, they're all grown-up, they live in Brooklyn. I think, They'll calm me down somehow.

I hold out the picture. I say, "Look! Look at this!"

And these two New York City girls, these girls who have seen everything, say, "*What the hell?*"

They have no idea what to think either.

Then Desiree remembers something: It's a fad, a teen-age thing. She's heard about it. Boys are sending around pictures of their penises that they have taken using their iPhones. (This was so new it wasn't called sexting yet; there wasn't even a word for it.)

Desiree says those numbers I saw on the in-box are actually the boy's iPhone number.

My older daughter says, "It's probably just some boy she knows, some boy just trying to be funny."

I want to know. I want to hear the voice of the boy who's trying to be funny—or whatever he's trying to be. I want him to know I know.

I call the iPhone number.

"Hello?" It's a teenage boy's voice. He says "Hello?" warily; I figure he doesn't recognize my phone number on his iPhone screen.

"Hi! Who's this?"

"M——," he says, giving his name. Good Lord, this boy would probably follow a guy who said he had a hurt puppy in his car. I have this parental urge to say, "You don't have to give me your name, I'm a stranger. You don't have to tell me anything." But I don't.

"Hi, M! This is R's mother."

"Who?"

"R. Are you a friend of hers?"

"I guess. Kinda."

"Where do you go to school?" He tells me, silly boy. It's not my daughter's school. It's a school in her school's neighborhood, and she does know some kids there, but I meet most of the kids she hangs out with, I hear their names over and over, and his name hasn't come up once. I'm pretty sure she doesn't know him that well. On the other hand, if I do decide to exact retribution, it will now take me about three minutes, just from the information he has given me, to find out who he is and what his parents' home phone number is.

"I see," I say. "I was just calling because your phone number showed up on my cell phone and I didn't know who'd called me."

Long pause. "Oh."

And I think, He's putting it together. He knows.

I say, "Okay, well, nice talking to you. Bye."

And he says, "Bye." He could have hung up on me, but he's polite. He's talking to a grown-up.

So. This seems to be a boy my girl kind of knows who is indulging in a disgusting fad. It's disgusting, but it's so disgusting it suddenly seems funny. Also, I'm so relieved that the possible other, darker scenario isn't true—we are not going to be a statistic in *Newsweek*, it seems—that I'm practically giddy. My older daughter and Desiree and I spend the next few minutes laughing about M and his member and the conversations we might have with him about it if we meet him.

I hear the front door open. It's my younger daughter,

home from school. I'm still rattled by the picture, but now I feel panicky; I'm about to be busted. I've been reading her e-mail, I've printed it out, and she is going to kill me.

I think, Don't make this some heavy thing. Be light, be light.

What's my choice? We're all standing here with these big grins frozen on our faces.

She comes into the room and says, "What?" She wants to be in on the joke.

"Honey, I saw this e-mail in your in-box." I show her the picture.

"It's so gross!" She's giggling.

"Do you know this boy?"

"Barely. I met him, like, twice."

"Well, what's his point, really? Is he trying to be funny? Does he want to be your boyfriend?"

"I don't know! He's an idiot! Why are you reading my e-mail?" She's smiling, though, so I know she will forgive me.

In the days that follow, M and his penis are reduced to a funny anecdote in our family, included in the category of penis humor that my girls and their friends have honed over the years (a penis ditty, the product of a long car ride in Italy: "Wanahini wanahini, hello, is that your penee? Wanahini wanahini, does it drive a Lamborghini?").

I try to keep what M did down at fad status: just funnin', a latter-day version of streaking or mooning or skinny-dipping at rock concerts. All of these activities involved nudity and exhibitionism and flaunting your privates, didn't they? What's the difference between that and sending a picture of your penis over the phone?

This interpretation refuses to sit right. Those other fads were all about being with other people; they were convivial, they were group romps. I think of M alone in his bathroom, looking at Mom's bras and the dirty towels on the floor, taking pictures of his lonesome penis. Get out of there, boy! Go outside and get some air!

But just as grieving has its stages, I now enter a new stage of reacting to seeing a penis picture in a child's e-mail. I have passed through Shock, Panic, Hilarity, Pity; now, finally—what took me so long?—I enter Outrage. My God, it is not all right to send a picture of an erect penis to a thirteen-year-old. I can't believe how many days it has taken me to get exercised about this. She has seen pictures of penises before, but this one was personal, this one was meant for her. This one was in big, veiny close-up. Why didn't I say to M, when I had him on the phone, "Don't you ever send a picture of your penis to anyone again! I will send you to juvie!"

"Honey," I say to my younger daughter one day when we are on vacation in the country, "were you shocked when you saw the picture?"

"Yes." She's smiling, but she says "Yes" in the same tone that she might say "Of course" or "Duh."

"Well, what he did was send an assault, and that's wrong, and—"

"Bye-bye." She walks outside. She has always been a private person; she hates Talks. I bring it up two more times, but I'm rebuffed.

One afternoon I see her at the far corner of the yard, swinging on the swing set. Her older sister did the same thing when she was a teenager, on the swing set we'd bought for her when she was little. She'd go out there and swing back and forth, rocking herself into a kind of reverie.

Ten years later, the new baby came, and we bought a wooden swing set to replace the rusty old metal one. And now she has the same habit as her sister. Now, when there is absolutely nothing else to do, she goes out there and swings slowly, the wood making little creaking sounds like a sailboat's mast in the sea.

I watch her. Has she forgotten about M's penis? Will she ever?

She's not telling.

Back and forth, back and forth, my baby swings and swings.

IT'S ABOUT TIME

I live alone. These things happen. Your children grow up, your husband leaves, and then you are one. This is a happy story, I promise, but I do need to say this: Get ready. You may be next. And if you are, please, please try to remember what I am telling you now: You know how you never have enough time? You will have it. The very thing, that precious, out-of-reach, shimmering pot of gold you have been longing for. You will even have time *on your hands*. If you are wise, you will see it as a gift. If you are like me, you will have to do some stumbling around to get there.

Like so much in life, this story is about dinner. Dinner was how I spent almost thirty years of my life—shopping for dinner, making dinner, and eating dinner with my family. Slipping chopped carrots into the meat loaf so that more vegetables would be represented in the meal. Guiding dinner-table conversation so that it held something loftier than burp jokes. And then, after dinner, helping with homework, making sure children went to bed at a relatively decent hour.

It was the life I had chosen, and most of the time I loved it. It was domestic. It was cozy. So when this ritual ended, I was totally unprepared for the expanse of time that stretched out in the evenings.

With a few exceptions, I hadn't spent an evening alone since my twenties. I think that one of the reasons I got married in the first place was because I hated living alone, hated walking home after work past well-lit apartments where families were having what I assumed, longingly, to be their snug and happy evenings. I hated unlocking the door of my apartment, where it was pitch-dark, knowing that I'd be alone until the sun came up.

After I got married and had children, every single evening was accounted for. I loved that. And now, all these years later, I had this huge hole of time in the evenings again, this giant, gaping Grand Canyon of time. Nothing was expected of me. Good Lord, what was I supposed to do?

At first, I couldn't shake the feeling, hardwired after all those years, that I should be home. The light would fade at dusk, and I'd think, I'm supposed to be home, I'd better get home before dark. I missed my children and wondered what they were having for dinner. They didn't ever call me to say, "Oh, Mommy, I really miss your dinners." I wondered, petulantly, why I hadn't just ordered takeout all those years, and I regretted every judgmental thought I'd had about mothers who'd done exactly that.

But sometimes, when I'd remember I had no reason to go home, I'd go to the movies instead. The freedom of being able to do this, even if it felt strange at first (A movie on a weeknight? Was that allowed?), even if I felt self-conscious buying my solo ticket and sitting in my solo seat, thrilled me, the way I imagine astronauts feel when they're floating weightlessly in space.

Or I'd take the newspaper (another thing I finally had time for) and go to my favorite neighborhood coffee shop for its excellent turkey burger and coleslaw—again, feeling this freedom from not having to think about, shop for, and prepare a meal. I thought about the hours I'd spent doing these things—two or three hours a day, for decades—and I thought, Boy, that was a lot of hours. I could have read a book, or a thousand.

I realized I had the thing that people, including me, constantly bemoan that they have none of. Having no time, and complaining about it, is the norm. "I'll call you when I'm out from under," we tell each other, and then we don't, because we're never out from under. I'm not sure why we all think we're supposed to be too busy, or who started it. Go to Europe and you see people loafing around most of the day.

For many years, when a friend would phone me in the evening and ask, "Do you have a minute?," I'd think, meanly, No, actually, I don't. Later tonight I may have a minute, after I finish dinner and getting my children to bed, but I hope to be sleeping by then.

And now I had a minute. I had many minutes, entire evenings of minutes. I started to think of having time not as an oddity, or something to feel strange about, but as a kind of present that had been dropped in my lap. It seemed unbecoming, as my mother would say, to not enjoy the very thing that I'd been longing for all these years. It seemed kind of asinine, in fact.

I made myself call friends I'd promised to call years ago. I think they were surprised to hear from me—"Is everything all right?" one college friend asked. "Did somebody die?"—but they were nice about not reminding me that I'd been out of touch. Some of them had gotten divorced or remarried since I'd seen them, some had had cancer and I felt terrible that I hadn't known, but not one of them made me feel worse about it. I made dates to meet them for coffee and kept the dates, and I looked at pictures of their now-grown children on their cell phones and showed them pictures of mine. I visited friends who'd had operations and were stuck in bed. Other friends invited me to watch their adult children play in bands in tiny clubs downtown, and I went (loud, but fun). I tried to show up for people.

I tried stretching out time instead of filling it. For many weeks I acted in a play, and after the play I'd walk for a half hour or so before getting on the subway home. I loved those walks—decompressing, thinking about how the show went, feeling the freshness of the air after being in a stuffy theater for hours.

I came to look forward to eating alone. Does that sound like I'm protesting too much? I hope not. But really, it was a surprising relief not to have to keep up dinner-table conversation, to make sure that everyone got asked (and congratulated for!) what they did that day. I made friends with the prepared-food section of my grocery store, an area I'd mostly shunned ("I can make that!"), and I tried out everything in it, even the green salads it would have taken me five minutes to throw together at home.

MADE BY MARIA, say the labels on the carrot-and-mango salad, cranberry chicken salad. I don't know who Maria is—the deli man says she's Greek and cooks for several stores—but I love her food, which I usually eat on a tray in bed while watching some detective show. I take a long bath, so long that my fingertips wither, and then I get in bed with my tray, and I send a little telepathic thank-you to Maria, wherever she may be, for making my delicious dinner. Sometimes I call my children, and sometimes they call me, and we catch up. But sometimes it's just me. That's fine too.

TAKE MY HOUSE, PLEASE

Friends!

Happy New Year to you all! Please forgive the mass e-mail, but I hope you'll read on. I have a terrific idea, and I hope you agree.

It's never too early to think about vacation plans, and I've been thinking about yours. Why not take your vacation on Martha's Vineyard this summer? At my house! I've decided to rent it, and I'm excited to tell you a little bit about it here.

I've been working like crazy to get the house in shape for you. I remind myself of Frank Sinatra when he ran around having his Palm Springs place spruced up for President Kennedy's visit—I'm all "Spare no expense!" and "I want those doorknobs to *shine*!" Unlike Frank, I am yelling at myself, but I like to pretend I have a staff like he did, just for fun. Also, I'm counting on a happy ending. The president never came to Frank's estate because of Frank's Mob connections, but I don't have any Mob connections. (Which

I'm kind of sad about, by the way. I'd love to have some stories to tell.) So come!

Anyhoo, I do have one helper. His name is Chet, and he's my handyman. And by *my* I mean "everyone's" handyman. Chet has a lot of other customers because none of the other handymen here show up, but Chet has a heart as big as all outdoors and does his best to fit me into his schedule. By the way, if Chet shows up to finish de-molding the walls while you're here, please invite him to stay for dinner. Most of his other customers are loaded and pay him a lot more than I do, so meals are the least I can offer. You'll like Chet; he has good stories. Ask him about the time he had to saw a hole in the wall here at my house to get at some smoking electrical wires. That's a good one.

I'm a divorcée now, which sounds kind of sexy and naughty, doesn't it? Like someone sashaying through a cocktail party in a spandex dress and three-inch heels, looking for someone's husband to steal. In fact, the correct translation of *divorcée* is "person with no money." Even if I went in for stealing other women's husbands, who has time? I'm way too busy digging through the sofa cushions for loose change, and eyeing the bits of silver here and there—a picture frame, my children's engraved baby cups—wondering if I can sell them as is or whether I have to melt them down first.

But enough about my troubles!

My house is a sweet old shingled farmhouse, with two "real" bedrooms and a cute little one off the kitchen that I'm guessing, from a certain earthy smell on humid days, used to be a milking shed, or a pigsty. We have two full bathrooms, except that the shower in the upstairs bathroom doesn't work. The shower per se works, but something's wrong with the drain, so water from the shower leaks down to the kitchen ceiling below, and then pours onto the floor. So limit yourselves to that downstairs shower, okay? Thanks much!

You're probably thinking that the house sounds like it's on the smallish side, but you don't want to stay in one of those new giant houses the rich people build here now. They're just gross. They're vulgar. You could fly a helicopter in those living rooms. You feel like a dwarf standing in them. You want to *rusticate*, am I right? You want your vacation to be real. Old-fashioned, a little funky, but real. Summer living the way it used to be, before the billionaires got here and discovered that if they said "lap pool," someone would build it for them.

Things you need to know when you get here:

- The trash cans, and the washing machine and dryer, are in the toolshed to the left of the kitchen door. Chet replaced some of the old beams holding up the shed's roof this winter because it was sagging pretty badly, and he's almost done now, but if you hear a lot of hammering in the night, that's him, fitting the job into his schedule. Try to avoid walking right under the old beams, though. Some bug or worm has eaten away at them, and now they have these daggerish shards of wood jutting out, and you'll get a big splinter in your head. If you do, just go to the emergency room.

- I think Chet has found all the rusty nails sticking out of the wooden stairs to the house, but Chet— he's funny, he cracks me up—calls trying to find them "whack-a-nail": Just when you think you've banged them all down, another one pops up. If you step on one of the popped-up ones by accident, promise me you'll go to the emergency room for a tetanus shot, okay?

- Apropos the toilet. Big favor: if the toilet doesn't flush, do *not* call Jim, our wonderful plumber. You need to save your calls to the plumbers here for important things; if you call them for every little problem, they look at their cell phones, see your number, and say, "Would you look who's calling *again*?" and turn them off. To fix the toilet, all you have to do is open up the tank. You know that big bulb that's attached to a rod? At the other end of the rod is a little wire loop we rigged up that should hold the rod on to the hook that connects to the metal stick that connects to whatever makes the toilet flush.

　　When the toilet doesn't flush, it means that the little piece of wire has broken. Just cut some more wire from the spool of wire that's somewhere in the toolshed and make another loop. It's easy. In the time it's taken you to read this paragraph, you could've done it twice, that's how cinchy it is.

• It takes a little longer to clean out the downstairs shower nozzle, but please don't call Jim for that, either. If the spray coming out of the nozzle is more like a trickle, it means that calcium or lead or what-not from the old pipes has clogged the little nozzle holes. Just take a pin and poke at those hundred or so holes until they're clear. Presto, the water flow will be full and robust again.

• If the water coming out of the faucets looks rusty or tastes funny, it's time to change the water filter. Get a new filter from the toolshed—they look just like paint rollers, and I think they're in the corner, in that heap of paint rollers—and go down to the pit under the house that holds the furnace.

    You get to the pit by lifting the trapdoor cut into the floorboards in the hallway. The trapdoor weighs a ton, so watch your fingers; also, crouch down when you go down the stairs into the pit, because the ceiling's about three feet over your head and you'll get a nasty gash if you hit it. If you're not already going to the emergency room for something else, you'll have to make another trip there.

The water-filter holder is an old glass cylinder, and all you have to do is screw it off from its holder, take out the sludge-covered old filter, and replace it with the new one. You know what? I think you'll like this job. I do. It makes you feel good knowing that no one in your family is drinking poisoned water anymore.

• Speaking of water, sometimes this oily black water escapes from our old cast-iron radiators and forms little puddles on the floor. You know what's crazy? It does this in the summer as well as in the winter, and in the summer we're not even using the radiators. Go figure! Anyway, make sure you blot up the oily water with a paper towel before any pets start lapping at it (pet emergency room).

• Don't flush either toilet when anyone is taking a shower or the shower water will turn boiling hot (emergency room).

• Don't use the dishwasher when you're using the washing machine. Doing this seems to confuse the pipe that delivers hot water to both machines, and it will deliver only frigid water to both; also, both machines will refuse to progress to the rinse cycle.

• Don't use the washing machine and the dryer at the same time. This overtaxes the wall outlet they share and may cause a small explosion (emergency room).

- Don't use the shower or the dishwasher or the washing machine or the kitchen faucet or the outdoor hose or the toaster while you're running a bath, or none of them will work. You know what? Just to make life simpler? Don't take a bath.

- Re: the toaster, the little lever on it doesn't stay down while you're toasting, so just stand there and hold it down manually until your toast is done, which takes about fifteen minutes. You won't mind—you're on vacation, right?

- Please be supercareful of the windows in the bedrooms. They've lost the springs that help them open and shut. We prop them open with those old hardcover John Gunther volumes you'll see on the floor nearby. If you remove the books, make absolutely sure that none of your fingers are under the window when it slams down (emergency room).

- Our boiler is very flatulent, especially in the dead of night, but nothing's wrong with it. You'll get used to the rumblings; they won't even wake you up after your fourth or fifth night.

    That reminds me. Sometimes the house will make a thudding sound, a big *thunk*. It's disconcerting. I always run around like one of the less successful Three Little Pigs, looking for which side of the house has fallen off.

Not to worry: Chet says this is just the house "settling." It's 150 years old—you'd think it would be settled by now! But Chet says this happens with old houses, especially the ones that don't have a real foundation.

Our house stands on top of a few stubby ancient brick columns, and boulders scrounged long ago from a field. The boulders and columns have shifted in recent years, which you can tell by the various swells in the downstairs floors. Especially in the living room, where there's a big bulge right in the middle of the room. That's because one of the boulders is sticking up pretty far now.

Chet's doing me a huge favor and promises to finish working on the whole boulder/column situation while you're here. He's been at it since February, working under the house. I never know exactly what he does down there, but he's using a professional sander. After he's been at it a few hours, there's a film of white dust, which comes up through the cracks in the old floorboards, over all the downstairs furniture, and all over Chet, who crawls out covered in white, like a ghost, or like he's just survived an explosion in a chalk factory.

If he's working while you're here, just wipe the dust off the furniture. Chet doesn't seem to mind the dust, so you don't have to wipe him off.

But you might want to keep any easily startled small children at a distance.

• We have our own underground well and a pump to supply our water. Isn't that neat? But sometimes the pipe running from the well to the house gets a crack in it, and a little geyser bubbles up onto the backyard.

Okay, here I go again: Don't call Jim. This is a job for the pump people. By the time they get here, in a few days or weeks, the pond will have become its own little ecosystem, with frogs hopping in and out and mosquitoes skating over its surface. Some people call this "standing water" and warn against it, nervous about the mosquitoes carrying diseases. I say it's a pond, and enjoy it.

We also have our own cesspool, installed before modern septic tanks were even a glimmer in someone's eye. The upside about cesspools is that you don't have to have them pumped regularly, the way you have to do with septic tanks. The bacteria in the cesspool magically work to break down all the waste that goes into it. Cool, right?

The downside, at least at our house, is that every few years you'll hear a gurgling sound coming from the kitchen sink. Or you'll smell something unpleasant wafting from that direction. This means that a wad of toilet paper (use sparingly!) has clogged the pipe to the cesspool, and waste matter is finding its way into the sink. Please don't panic.

This is what plungers are for! I keep ours right there in the kitchen, next to the trash can, for just this reason.

If, after a couple of hours of plunging, the sink is still filling up, call the number I keep next to the phone. It's for Jim. Now's the time to call him.

FAKING IT

Every morning, I face my e-mail as if it were a firing squad. I'm so scared of what might be there that I have failed or forgotten to do or will not be able to do, thereby disappointing or angering someone. I'm scared of the phone and of the regular mail for the same reason, although less so, only because hardly anyone I know under eighty uses the phone or real mail anymore.

You'd think I would have overcome this fear by now. I've been in therapy! I know how to meditate! But you know what, honestly? I think I can hope for some improvement, but if I were going to get better about it, I probably would be by now.

I'm not frightened about things I should be scared of—choking on a piece of steak or getting bedbugs from clothes I buy in thrift shops or getting rear-ended by a texting soccer mom. I'm aware that these things might happen to me, but I figure I'll worry about them when they do.

What I'm scared of, if it has a theme, is letting people

down: Somewhere, someone is or is about to be mad at me, or hurt—and the e-mail/regular mail/phone call is going to be the agent of this terrible turn of events. I forgot to go to a friend's party or write a letter of recommendation or watch her web series. I've failed her, or I'm about to.

Sometimes, of course, I do mess up. Sometimes people *are* mad at me. I got a frosty e-mail recently from a woman I know, taking me to task for not calling her more often; last week I got a polite-but-fed-up e-mail from the guy who installed a new water tank in my basement three months ago, reminding me of the bill I'd forgotten to pay.

But I don't get those e-mails that often. When my friends haven't heard from me in a while, they generally send sweet e-mails asking if I'm okay. If I've forgotten to reply to an e-mail promptly, people are usually understanding. But that doesn't seem to matter to me. I dread opening the e-mails anyway. I even suspect that underneath their understanding tone, my friends are, in fact, angry or upset or crushed. This is how pathetic I am: Sometimes I get e-mail overdue-book notices from my local library and imagine that Beth, the head librarian, is mad at me, even though I know, from personal experience, that Beth is never mad about it. All Beth ever says, even when you return a book two years late, is, "This is great. Thank you. And if you could bring in a few cans of something for the food bank, we'll just forget about the fine."

But of course I have to answer the e-mails, the phone, the regular mail. (I'm trying with Facebook, but I'm sorry, it's like being in hell to me, the equivalent of answering a knock at the door to find five hundred people there, all talking at once.) So I make myself do it. I ape the words of other people, people who, unlike me, seem to face their communications without terror. *Will you take a rain check?* I type, and *I might be able to do it after the New Year* or *Sorry about delayed response!* But I'm totally faking the lightheartedness. Inside I'm dying a little, every time.

There's a saying in AA (they have a saying for everything in AA) about following the program even if you don't get it at first: "Fake it till you make it." I have been faking it forever.

I would like to be able to say that all this faking it is paying off—that I'm getting less anxious. I do experience an almost drunken exhilaration when I've finished a session of answering e-mails (notice I didn't say "when I'm done with e-mail," because you're never, ever done with it—ten more e-mails have poured in while you're answering one, which is just evil), a euphoric relief as out of proportion as the dread. And sometimes an e-mail brings good news—every day I hear from people I love, and sometimes people offer to pay me to write or perform something, which is wonderful. But the exhilaration never lasts. The next day I'm filled with dread all over again.

My dream is to be like my friend Debra, who responds to my occasional e-mails asking how she is a week or two after I send them. She never apologizes. I wouldn't want her to, because I never get mad. I know I'll hear from her sooner or later; I know if I e-mailed her about some dire or urgent thing, she'd e-mail me right back. I love her lack of guilt. I wish I could bottle it and drink it. But for now, faking it will have to do.

CAN I BORROW THAT?

You know how no one's making kitten heels this year? It's so weird—last year every shoe was a kitten heel, and now all the heels are like stilts again. I'm like, "Denise, you dodo, you should've bought ten pairs!" And now I can't find the one pair I had. I think my cleaning lady took them. So can I borrow your alligator ones? Just put them by your front door in a plastic bag in case it rains. I'll swing by as soon as I get a minute.

You know what? Can you throw your black push-up bra in there too? I don't know what happened to mine (cleaning lady, probably!). I'll return yours as soon as I replace it. That's a promise.

Oh, can I borrow that handheld gizmo you have that steams the milk for coffee right in the cup? I'm going to make my famous blondies if I have time, and they go great with cappuccino. I'll give you some of the blondies so you can see how yummy they taste together.

You know your convection oven? I'd love to use it, just for the blondies. Hold on—I can get the steamer thing when I come over to use the convection oven. Duh! Don't worry if you can't find your big spatula after I leave—I need to use it for the blondies, but I'll take it home with me because I think it might actually be mine.

Speaking of appliances, can I borrow that Jack LaLanne juicer you bought when you were on Ambien? It's probably still in the box at your house, but I'd use it all the time if I had it. I'll make you some arugula juice—it's bitter, but it totally cleans you out—but you might have to remind me. I'm really busy.

Guess what? For a trade, you can borrow my wok. Scratch that—it's a present! Just take off the black crusty stuff in the bottom with Brillo or a knife or something. Guess what else? You can have my garlic roaster too—not to borrow, to keep. I'm not sure where it is, so I might have to give it to you later.

·

Can I borrow your lawn mower? Just the machine, not the guy. Well, the guy too, but only if he gets done at your house early.

Can I have your beach house? For that week when you're going to Umbria? This way you won't have to worry about people breaking in and "squatting" in it while you're away. People do that. And sometimes they get stoned and use the owner's furniture for bonfires. It's a trend. I read about it in the paper.

Can I borrow some of your frequent-flier miles to get to the beach? JetBlue is running a promotion, so it only costs 237,000 miles to fly there. The offer expires in about three minutes, so get back to me *right away*, sistah, okay?

Go to my Kickstarter page to see what I'll be working on while I'm at the beach. I know my project sounds a little like your project, but I'm going to do mine in a different way. With puppets, and much more cement.

It takes about two seconds to become a donor on my Kickstarter page. After you do it, forward the link to all of your friends, and tell them that if they don't become donors in the next twenty-four hours, bad fortune will visit them. Don't scare them, just mention it.

If I don't have time to make the blondies, just forget about the convection oven and the cappuccino thing. I do still need the kitten heels and the bra, though, and the spatula.

BTW, is your husband good with machines? My printer needs a new toner cartridge, and I can't remember how to put it in. You know what? Just send him over later with the cartridge, and an extra one if you have it, and the juicer, and my spatula. And the bra and the heels, and two martini glasses and some small green olives. I'll be home all evening.

You know what? Send him with that Wedgwood dessert plate too. If I have time to make my famous fudge, I'll send him home with some on the plate. You can return the plate later, no problem.

MY GRATITUDES

Sometimes I forget to do my Gratitudes, and that's just dumb.

Because when we don't take the time each day to count our Gratitudes, our Ingratitudes just rush right in and take over. And then we are off to the fucking races, are we not? Life seems to hold nothing but the many unfortunate, heartbreaking, humiliating things that happen to us, sometimes in a single day, our existence merely an accretion of thousands upon thousands of those days, our only prospect an old age in which we are sure to get stranger and more ill-tempered by the minute until we finally die, alone and in diapers, leaving all of our money to two cats named Bosco and Archduke Vladimir von Furstenkitty.

What I'm saying is that we can always find things to be thankful for, even the unluckiest among us. And it only takes a few minutes each day.

·

Some of your Gratitudes can be for things that have happened to you that are bad, but that you can "repurpose" into positives. For example, being a "permalancer" for a company that would rather blow itself up than hire you as a real employee. You're barely making a living wage, that's true, and you get no health benefits; on the upside—the Gratitude side—you do get to steal pretty much all the office supplies you want, and you're not invited to the interminable Friday-morning staff meetings where Ron takes up an hour bloviating about his dumb ideas.

Another example: No one except horny4U and hillbillygoat has favorited you on Match.com in, like, a month. Sad, in a way, but turn it around: If you did meet and marry someone, he'd probably turn out to be one of those men with a whole other family in another state. And you would be certain to find this out in some especially sickening way—you'd see a photo in the paper of a Little League team that won the regionals and think, My, that coach looks just like my Steve, or you'd be taking your kids on a little road trip, and you'd run into your husband and his other wife and their four children at a Denny's, laughing and eating pancakes.

You can also be Grateful that the bad things that have happened to you at least haven't happened to you again *today*. Like, I'm Grateful that today a ticket taker at the movie theater didn't ask me if I was a senior citizen and then, when I said no, say, "*Really?*" That was last week.

And once you put your Gratitudes thinking cap on, they just come at you, one after the other, like shiny presents on Christmas morning. Take something as simple as your name.

Maybe you don't like your name—it's bland or hard to pronounce—but at least you didn't have to grow up with a last name like Butts or Breasted or Hyman or Crotchly, or a first name that rhymes with vagina, such as Genina or Jemima or Regina. Although, if I were named Regina, I would definitely just lie and tell everyone it was pronounced *Regeena*.

Speaking of names, I'm Grateful every day not to know that I am a distant and yet blood relative of Hermann Göring, Kool-Aid cultist Jim Jones, Tiny Tim, or Rudolph Giuliani. This is because I never go on Ancestry.com, and I urge you to do the same. Going on Ancestry.com is just borrowing trouble, and who needs trouble when we are gathering our Gratitudes?

Apropos my health, I'm Grateful that I don't suffer from horrific "cluster" headaches, so excruciating they can drive their sufferers to suicide, and instead just have "tension" headaches, even if I have them, like, all day. And though I also suffer from a variety of other (digestive! don't ask!) ailments, a big shout-out of Health Gratitude for not sending me with a minor cut to the emergency room, there to contract a flesh-eating bacteria from the germ-soaked hospital air, requiring the grafting of skin from my buttocks onto my face. Merci, Gratitude gods, for that!

Okay, I wish I had a bigger apartment—who doesn't? But at least Robert Durst has not moved in across the hall and sought out my friendship by knocking on my door and asking to borrow one of my "frocks," right?

Also, since my apartment is a walk-up, there is no chance I will get stuck in a broken elevator for seven hours with a jonesing crystal meth addict and his increasingly peckish dog, a rottweiler/pit bull mix.

Apartment-wise, I'm also Grateful that five firemen didn't show up at my door just now and order me to evacuate the building because of a gas leak on my floor. I would have had to go outside in what I am wearing, an old chenille bedspread that I have turned into a "sarong" and a T-shirt that I think I used as a cleaning rag for a while, and stand around on the sidewalk while Con Ed fixed the problem. And then some street-fashion photographer would take my picture and publish it in one of those Fashion Do's and Don'ts columns, as the lead Don't.

You know what I'm so Grateful for? That I haven't been purposely tripped by one of those disturbing, mean cartoon characters in Times Square, a Smurf or a Minnie Mouse, sprained my shoulder in my fall, and then had all the cartoon characters gather round to heckle me while I lay sprawled on the street, my last memory before passing out from pain being snickered at by a dirty Ernie and a Teletubby.

As far as other public humiliations go, I am truly Grateful, today and every day, that I am not an unattractive eighth grader at a snobby private girls' school whose more popular classmates have decided to practice witchcraft on me by sticking pins into a doll they have given my name, and then tweeted about it. Some of the girls would invariably be the daughters of rich and famous parents, and their tweets, and my name, would become an item on Page Six of the *New York Post*, guaranteeing that I would be known forever as the loser who was tormented by amateur Wiccans.

I think that's about it for this morning's Gratitudes—I've totally turned around my outlook on the day, ready to face the endless crap that will come my way—except for my closing Gratitude, which I always try to give a Not Dead theme, to remind myself that just being alive is better than dying—or, certainly, dying gruesomely.

So today I am Grateful that I am not three-quarters of the way up Mount Everest, with a storm brewing at the peak and a cocky guide who, in spite of warnings from our Sherpas, has convinced our entire party that we should go for it. Bad, bad idea. I will spend my last moments on earth stumbling around on my frozen legs through blinding snow until I fall, fatally, into a chasm. It makes dying at home in diapers sound like—well, okay, not fun, but something to be, in a way, totally Grateful for.

MY NEW FEMINIST COP SHOW

I am so excited about *Bust*, my new TV show. It has a strong feminist slant and stars me, as homicide detective Casey O'Malley. Every week a woman gets murdered in some hideous, hair-raising fashion, and I relentlessly track down the perps—the rapists, the serial killers, the wife beaters, the sex traffickers, the victims' creepy gynecologists and professors and fitness trainers, their incestuous dads, sadistic pimps, pervy ministers, and sketchy neighbors.

I find these monsters and I spit in their faces—*ptui!*—when they try to flirt with me while I interrogate them. Then I rip their lame alibis to shreds. "Oh, you're gonna do time all right," I say. "A *lot* of time. You're gonna die in your cell of old age, my friend, unless you're lucky enough to have someone on the inside stick a shiv in you first. 'Cause you know what you have to look forward to otherwise? That's right, the shower. Plenty of guys who'll be happy to get a piece of even *your* sorry ass."

In short, I speak for all the women in this corrupt cess-pool of a woman-hating world that objectifies us and treats us like pieces of meat. I empower women with my kick-ass avenging-angel feminist goodness.

All right, yes, there appear to be completely different dress codes for me and for the men in my department. While I, Casey, wear extremely tight, low-slung blue jeans and deep-V-neck T-shirts out of which my abundant cleavage swells, or tank tops that accidentally ride up to show my taut midriff, my brilliant partner, Josh Aronowitz, and the other detectives I work with wear neckties, button-down shirts, and boxy suits. It doesn't matter where I am—a funeral for one of my vics, a black-tie opening at the opera where my sicko billionaire suspect has a box—there I am in skintight jeans and skimpy tops. And no one ever says, "Don't you have any work clothes?" or "What, are we doing Casual Tuesdays now?"

Recently, I mentioned to Craig, our show's creator and showrunner, that I felt a little funny about this. "But haven't you noticed that you always get to the perp just a moment before Josh and the other guys?" he replied. "That's because all those baggy clothes slow them down, like sails in the wind."

He's right. I do always get to the perp first. Which is appropriate, since it's up to me to be awesome on behalf of all women. So I'm glad Craig cleared that up.

Another thing that used to make me uncomfortable is how sometimes on the show I don't even get skimpy outfits—I'm just in my underwear. Like, in one episode,

I confuse the men's and women's locker rooms at the station and Josh comes in right as I'm stripping down to my lacy bra and panties.

And even though Josh is brilliant and erudite and a total egghead (his parents are Nobel Prize–winning physicists, but he has chosen to go into police work, bless him), he is nonetheless a flesh-and-blood man, and this moment of powerful sexual chemistry between us is even more piquant because we cannot give in to it. It would distract us from our work.

I asked Craig if these scenes are just a way to show me with hardly any clothes on, and to lure viewers into watching our show in the hope that Josh and I will eventually get it on. He sighed deeply and shook his head. "I didn't think I'd have to spell this out," he said. "As you know, you, Casey, often toil through the night, drinking the crappy station-house coffee and looking at thousands of mug shots in pursuit of your perp. In the morning, you have to shower at work because you don't have time to go home, but you're so tired that sometimes you get the men's and women's rooms mixed up. We're showing our viewers the obsessive devotion that makes you a hero to women everywhere. Got it?"

"I do! So that explains why I'm wearing just a filmy nightie in those scenes when Josh comes to my apartment in the middle of the night to tell me about some development in the case that he could have just texted me about?"

"Exactly right. You're always on duty."

"But I can't help noticing that Josh keeps looking at my nightgown like he wants to see what's under it."

"Oh, ignore that. That's just a guy thing."

That was a relief. But one other thing was kind of bothering me. I couldn't help noticing that almost all of the women who get murdered on our show are attractive, even gorgeous, and young, hardly ever over, say, thirty years old. And a lot of them seem to be fresh-faced-yet-nubile teenagers.

"Do ugly women ever get murdered?" I asked Craig one day. "Or fat women, or old ladies?"

"Sometimes, but not that often. Believe me, if they did, we'd show it."

That made me feel much better. For a moment there, I'd thought Craig was trying to get away with something.

SCARY STORIES FOR GROWN-UPS

ON HOLD

"No, I would *not* like to call back later," Ellen Krugman said grumpily to the Time Warner Cable customer-service representative on the other end of the line. "I did that yesterday with someone there named Richard, but when I tried to call him back at the extension he gave me, there was no such extension. And when I called customer service again, they said no one there was named Richard. So no, I'm not calling back, thank you very much. I'm staying on hold."

"Please wait while I speak with my supervisor," said the representative. "I'm sorry if there has been any inconvenience."

If? thought Ellen. There had been a *lot* of inconvenience. For the third month in a row, Ellen had been billed not the $59 for the "special package" of phone, cable, and Internet service that she had signed up for, but for separate and "premium" monthly charges for phone, cable, and the

Internet, plus late-payment charges, and $54 for a three-year subscription to *Sports Illustrated for Kids*—$3,489 in all. Ellen had called every month, to no avail. Normally a mild-mannered, easy-going sort, Ellen was now at the end of her rope. "I'll do whatever it takes to clean up this darned mess once and for all," she said to herself.

Hours passed while Ellen languished on hold. Night fell. Fearing she might doze off, she downed cup after cup of black coffee, requiring frequent trips to the bathroom, and much running of the water in the sink so the person at the other end—if there was ever going to be a person at the other end—wouldn't suspect she was using the toilet. Ellen took to just chewing the coffee beans, a fistful at a time.

Dawn broke. Ellen was still on hold. Night fell again. And again. True to her vow, Ellen stayed on hold, chewing on her coffee beans, for five days. Floaters began to dance in front of her eyes, which she believed to be undetonated hand grenades sent by the cable company, and she dashed frantically around her apartment in an effort to catch them. Finally, Ellen's downstairs neighbor, alarmed by the sounds of Ellen's body slamming against the walls, brought her to Bellevue Hospital. Ellen was diagnosed with a psychotic break and consigned to the psych ward. There she remains to this day, huddled in a corner of the bile-yellow rec room, clutching her now-antique flip phone, still waiting, still hoping, still on hold.

THE HITCHHIKER

"Need a lift?" said the driver, his face shrouded by the wide brim of a handsome black Stetson.

Normally, sensible thirty-year-old Maeve Slingerland wouldn't accept a ride from a stranger, even a friendly sounding old fellow like the one in the shiny black Range Rover that had pulled up alongside her. But she needed a ride, badly. She had to get help right away for Jeff, her fiancé.

Two weeks earlier, she and Jeff had struck out high-spiritedly from Manhattan in Jeff's beat-up old Volvo, camping their way across the country en route to Maeve's college roommate's wedding in San Francisco. They'd had a fine, trouble-free time—until now.

Shortly after crossing into Montana, she and Jeff had ventured down a dirt road looking for a picturesque campsite. They were delighted when they found that the road led to a babbling, crystal-clear creek at the foothills of the majestic Rockies. No sooner had they pitched their tent, however, than Jeff complained of feeling hot and dizzy. Using her emergency-kit thermometer, Maeve was alarmed to find that it registered Jeff's temperature at 104 degrees—and climbing.

"Off we go!" said Maeve, struggling to sound upbeat. "Let's find a doctor to take a look at you." Ashen-faced and trembling, Jeff could only nod in assent.

But when Maeve turned the key in the ignition, the Volvo wouldn't start. Again and again she tried, but it was no use. The old car's engine refused to turn over.

To make matters worse, Maeve's cell phone, she discovered, wasn't getting a signal at their remote spot. She had only one option: to set off on foot, promising Jeff to return with help as soon as she could.

For two long, hot hours Maeve had walked the dirt road back in the direction of the highway with not a single car in sight. At last she'd reached a more trafficked road—but the few cars that passed had ignored her outstretched thumb.

Now, with the appearance of the man in the Range Rover, her luck seemed to have changed. "If you're heading to town," said the old gent, "hop on in."

Gratefully, Maeve climbed into the passenger seat.

"Where do you hail from?" asked the driver.

"New York City."

"New York! That's one of your blue states, isn't it?" The old man's voice had taken on a cool, almost hectoring tone; Maeve saw two thin lips curled into what looked like a smirk. A strange, but somehow familiar, sneer. She'd seen it before, she was certain.

"I guess," said Maeve warily.

"You *guess*?"

"I don't really follow politics." In fact, Maeve had majored in Geogender Political Cinema Studies at Mount Holyoke and now worked at Planned Parenthood, but she didn't want any trouble.

"You know what, missy? I don't believe you." With that, Maeve heard the ominous thudding sound of the car doors locking.

"Here's what we're going to do: We're going to take a nice, long drive while I explain how American freedom will not be secured by empty threats, meaningless red lines, leading from behind, appeasing our enemies, abandoning our allies, or apologizing for our great nation."

On and on he fumed, spittle forming at the corners of his mouth. Suddenly, Maeve knew who he was.

But it was too late. Maeve was a prisoner in the car, which the man drove and drove down the winding country roads, ranting all the while, until darkness fell. At last they arrived at a huge, imposing house high on a mountain.

"Mommy!" the man called out his car window. "Come see what I brought!"

A small, stout woman in a knit suit appeared from the shadows. The man rolled down Maeve's window, and the woman reached in on Maeve's side, squeezing the flesh on Maeve's forearm between two fingers.

"Mmmm," said the woman. "Firm, but tender. Good hunting, Daddy. I'll just go preheat the oven."

Maeve had an idea. "Is that Valerie Jarrett?" she said, pointing into the darkness.

The man turned his head to look, a low, growling noise coming from deep in his throat. At that moment, Maeve reached across him, pressed the unlock button, flung open her door, tumbled out of the car, and ran for her life.

Eventually, after flagging down a ride from a state trooper, Maeve found a doctor in town, and they drove back to Jeff, whose fever, it turned out, was only a case of the flu.

When they arrived at the wedding, Maeve and Jeff couldn't wait to tell the other guests the amazing story of how Maeve had been abducted and almost eaten for dinner by Dick and Lynne Cheney. "You'll never believe this," Maeve began. But when she finished telling the story, everyone said they totally, totally believed it.

DUTCH BOY

Frieda Gleason was glad she'd treated herself to a weekend out of town. Hardworking and frugal, Frieda usually devoted her weekends to supplementing her modest proofreader's salary with freelance work. But if she hadn't gone this weekend to visit her childhood chum Peggy in Sag Harbor, she'd never have met Roger, the handsome real estate broker who'd sat down next to her, and with whom she was now having a long, lively chat on the Hampton Jitney.

Roger was the first man shy Frieda felt instantly comfortable with. As they talked, she discovered that they had the same likes and dislikes—both enjoyed early-morning walks in the park, disliked Joe Scarborough as well as Mika Brzezinski, and still read the paper version of the *Times*.

"Would you like to have dinner sometime?" Roger asked when they both got off the jitney at the Eighty-Sixth Street and Lexington Avenue stop. "I've always wanted to go to Per Se."

"Me too!" said Frieda, who had once proofread an article about the elegant eatery.

Several days later, the two of them sat down to dinner at the restaurant. Roger suggested the full nine-course tasting menu. "Would that be all right with you?"

How courteous, even courtly, he is, not to mention

generous, thought Frieda, who noticed that the tasting menu cost $325 per person.

Roger even splurged on a $250 bottle of Burgundy. "Should we?" he asked, smiling, before summoning the sommelier.

"Oh, why not?" Frieda replied, delighted. Most of her dates took her to restaurants they invariably advertised as "fun," meaning "cheap." Frieda had had her fill of Mexican and Indian joints. Here, at last, was a man willing to splurge on his date!

At the end of the sumptuous meal, the waiter brought the bill. "So we'll just split this down the middle," Roger said, placing his credit card next to it.

"Excuse me?" said Frieda.

"Well, technically you owe a little more—you had the latte—but it's not a big deal." Roger paused, then chortled. "Did you think I was paying for the whole thing?"

"Yes!"

"Why?"

"Because that's the rule. I don't know why!"

"That's stupid."

And that is how Frieda Gleason paid $458 for her dinner, not including tax and tip.

MINDFULNESS PAYS

The residents of Happy Lotus Sangha, a Buddhist community in upstate New York, were just sitting down to their noonday meal of black rice and beet greens when the door of the dining hall was flung open. There, standing in the doorway, was Martha Stewart herself!

The members of Happy Lotus, many of them former corporate executives and the like, recognized her straightaway. They'd heard that she'd bought the robber baron's estate next door, but none of them had expected the domestic diva to call on them.

Yet here she was —grinning broadly, a calico bandanna tied around her neck, and holding out a platter. On it was a large cake, its top an exquisite lotus flower crafted from hundreds of candied citrus-peel "petals."

"*Namaste*, gang!" she said. "Please enjoy this Meyerlemon cake. I made it myself, and it took me thirty-seven hours. But I've just retired, so I have more time. Speaking of time, you know what I'd like more of in my life from here on in? The kind of loving-kindness and compassion that you practice here at Happy Lotus. May I join you in your morning meditations?"

"Of course!" exclaimed the delighted Rinpoche. Wizened but robust, the ninety-seven-year-old Tibetan monk delighted in welcoming all guests to Happy Lotus, where residents lived a life of penury, eking out an existence from the sale of handmade meditation cushions and prayer flags.

And join them Martha did—chanting and meditating every day from dawn till noon, attending Rinpoche's daily dharma talks, and humbly taking her turn serving the others at mealtime.

One day, Martha failed to appear at the sangha. In the middle of morning meditation, there came a knock on the front door. When one of the sangha members answered it, a smiling, attractive woman stood in the doorway, flanked by a camera crew. "I'm Robin Roberts, from *Good Morning America*. We'd like to talk with Rinpoche about Martha's new Lovingkindness line, inspired by her time here with you."

Robin Roberts held out a handsome, slick catalog, filled with products: Here, in varieties of maroon and orange, Buddhism's colors, were meditation cushions and prayer flags as well as accent pillows, sheets, towels, duvet covers, dog beds, garden accessories, luggage, and Lovingkindness-ware, a collection of cookware and kitchen utensils.

Rinpoche, who had joined the sangha member at the door, perused the catalog. "Where is Martha?" he asked solemnly. "I must speak with her."

"She's in the Mojave Desert, getting ready to fly to outer space with Richard Branson," replied Robin Roberts. "Isn't that so Martha?"

Rinpoche walked briskly to Martha's mansion. There, on the expansive front lawn, he saw a sign: FOR SALE BY SOTHEBY'S INTERNATIONAL REALTY. The mansion's doors were locked, the shades drawn, the usual fleet of SUVs gone. Martha had moved on.

"Everything changes," Rinpoche comforted his followers. All life was impermanent, he reminded them, including Martha's.

Yet even Rinpoche found that he could not entirely overcome his negative emotions, particularly when *The Wall Street Journal* reported that Martha's Lovingkindness line had grossed $187 million in its first three months. Even monks get tired of eating rice every night.

THE ANNIVERSARY

Stacy Stengel had never felt so miserable.

She'd thought of the perfect way for her and Dave to celebrate their five-year anniversary: a romantic weekend getaway. And she had just the place—the rustic Vermont inn she found on the Internet. Photos showed spacious rooms with four-poster beds and fluffy duvets, and a dining room with a fire crackling in the hearth.

She knew that she and Dave badly needed some quality time together. Dave had been moody and irritable for so long—finding fault with everything she did, even going so far as to call her a "dummy" and "just a kindergarten teacher." Sometimes Stacy wondered if Dave even liked her anymore.

This weekend, Stacy thought, would surely do the trick. She and Dave would cuddle and laugh and get to know each other again.

At first, things had gone perfectly. Dave loved their dinner by the fireside, and had even made love to her afterward, albeit quickly, as was his habit.

Now, though, they were woken from their deep slumber by a noisy mayhem in the hallway—girlish screams and whoops of laughter, boyish bellows and hootings, and the unmistakable aroma of marijuana.

Stacy opened their door a crack. Here, like wild animals let out of their cages, were at least twenty teenagers, tearing up and down the corridor, pummeling and throwing things at each other.

"Would you please be quiet?" Stacy asked them.

"Uh . . . no?" said one of the boys, and back the mob went to their raucous carryings-on.

"What the fuck?" said Dave.

"The reservation clerk said there'd be a big group coming this weekend," said Stacy, crawling back into bed.

"And you didn't ask her what kind of group?" said Dave. "You can't be serious."

"I'm so sorry, Dave, I am!" said Stacy, her eyes shimmering with tears.

Stacy threw on her robe and went to the front desk. The night manager apologized profusely; the youngsters were from upstate New York, high school seniors on the school's annual ski trip. He had already complained to the trip's chaperones, but it had been no use; the scolded children had quieted down for a few minutes, but were soon up to their hijinks.

"We're leaving," said Dave, stuffing his clothes into his suitcase. He said not a word on the entire four-hour car ride home.

Soon Dave turned their anniversary weekend into a funny story, regaling all of their friends with the story of how the boisterous kids had ruined their stay, and how it was all Stacy's fault.

"Duh!" he would say, pointing at his wife. Stacy had never felt so humiliated.

Then one night, after having too many drinks at a buddy's bachelor party, Dave stripped off all his clothes and passed out in bed next to Stacy, who was lying awake, thinking about her marriage. Two hours later, needing to use the bathroom, he stumbled out of bed; still drunk, he took a wrong turn, mistook the front door of their apartment for the bathroom door, and ended up in the building's hallway.

"Stacy, let me in!" he pleaded as neighbors appeared at their doors, some cursing him for waking them, others giggling at his naked, shivering self. One neighbor took out a cell phone and shot a video of Dave yelling and banging on his door.

But Stacy didn't open the door.

The next morning, YouTube featured footage of Dave's misadventure, and by evening "Naked Dave" had fifteen million hits. Dave had become a global figure of fun.

Shortly thereafter, Dave and Stacy were divorced. Dave moved to Lapland, where he hoped (mistakenly, it turned out) that people hadn't heard of him. Stacy married a very nice man who thought she was adorable, and not dumb at all.

FERBERIZING

Phil and Janet Kriegler weren't surprised. Their daughter Giselle had always been an exacting, particular person, even bossy at times. So when she asked them to care for Jasper, her five-month-old, while she and her husband, Sam, attended her business school reunion, they knew she would have plenty of instructions for them.

Giselle gave Phil and Janet not a moment to recover from their five-hour journey, most of it on congested I-95, before she began going over her typed list of all the things they

needed to know to care for the baby. And none so important, Giselle stressed, as Jasper's "sleep program." Janet and
Phil looked at each other uneasily—they couldn't remember how any of their children had slept as infants. It was all
a blur.

"We've just begun Ferberizing him, and it's essential
that you enforce it," said Giselle, who felt that her parents
had been cavalier, even careless, in her own upbringing.

"Like Sanforizing!" said Phil playfully. "What is Sanforizing, anyway?"

Giselle ignored her father's remark. There was a time
for dopey jokes, and a time to be serious, Giselle felt, and
her dad had never known which was which.

Ferberizing, she explained, was a method of teaching
infants how to comfort themselves in their cribs so that
they could fall asleep on their own. When Jasper cried in
the night, Phil and Janet were allowed to go into his room,
but only to pat him and offer a few words of comfort before
leaving. Under no circumstances were they to pick him up.

"What we're aiming for is *gradual extinction*," said
Giselle.

"Like the dinosaurs!" said Phil.

"Oh, my God, would you *stop*," said Giselle. "*Gradual
extinction* means the slow removal of the parents from the
baby's room altogether."

The first night, Jasper cried when they put him in his
crib. They patted him and left the room. Jasper kept crying.
Phil got up, patted him, and went back to bed. Jasper cried.
Janet got up, patted him, and went back to bed. Jasper continued to wail. Phil got up. Then Janet got up. Then Phil got

up. Then Janet got up. On and on, until, with dawn breaking, all three of them finally fell into an exhausted sleep.

Phil said he'd rather be waterboarded than live through
another night of Ferberizing, but Janet wouldn't let him quit.

"That's it, we're done," Phil announced after the second night of nocturnal hell. Janet acceded, but only because
she had developed a ferocious migraine, her first in years.

For the rest of the week, Jasper slept in bed between
them. If he woke up in the night, Phil and Janet didn't notice. He seemed to quietly fall back asleep.

When Sam and Giselle returned, Phil and Janet, full of
false cheer, told them that Ferberizing had been a breeze.
Jasper had done great; they were practically extinct.

Three days later, Giselle called. "He cried all night!"
she told her mother. "He's worse than ever! He must be
regressing because we're home."

"I'm so sorry," said Janet.

A day later, Giselle called Janet again, even more agitated. "I just found one of his pacifiers at the foot of our
bed!" she said. "You and Daddy let him sleep with you!
I can't believe you lied to me!" Obviously, Giselle added,
she couldn't trust her parents to take care of their grandson
again.

"Hallelujah," said Phil, who could hear Giselle yelling
over the phone even though he was across the room.

"I heard that!" screamed Giselle. "I hate you!"

She'll get over it, Phil told Janet. But Giselle never did
get over it. She never left them alone with the baby again,
and she wouldn't bring Jasper to visit—she couldn't trust
them to childproof their home, she said. Janet and Phil

always had to go to Giselle's house to see Jasper. Phil said he almost preferred Ferberizing to driving on I-95, but there was nothing to be done about it. And in time, with Giselle's vigilant Ferberizing—seven and a half years of it, give or take—young Jasper learned to sleep through the night.

L.L.BEAN AND ME

I keep reading about how having cancer makes people appreciate their lives for the first time. I don't know, I think if it takes a life-threatening disease to make you appreciate your life, there may be something wrong with you. Needing cancer to appreciate your life is like needing a rock to fall on your head to appreciate gravity.

I found that having cancer made it harder to appreciate life. In a way, the surgeries and months of chemotherapy were straightforward: I was in crisis mode, my adrenaline was pumping, I was determined to sprint through it all with flying colors. What was harder was what came afterward—after the lovely nurses had waved me goodbye from the door of the chemo suite, after I got home and continued to feel like crap. The chemotherapy treatments left me tired for at least a year, long after the treatments were finished, so tired that I toyed with the idea of getting crutches just to prop me up while I stood. The chemicals had other unfortunate lingering side effects. My legs were pathetic—my joints ached, my muscles ached, the neuralgia buzzing through my nerves made my legs feel as if they'd been frozen and were just starting to thaw out, while being plugged into an electrical socket—a trifecta of pain that regularly reduced me to tears. I developed sharp, transient pains in my abdomen that convinced me I was sick again and would be dying shortly or, at my less anxious, made me wonder if my surgeon hadn't left a clamp or a slice of tubing behind during one of my operations. (A doctor finally said they were probably adhesions—post-surgical scarring—but not before other doctors had suggested bladder cancer or a prolapsed uterus, the latter offering the likelihood of a lifetime of pessary-wearing. Shoot me *now*, I thought.)

I knew that most patients with ovarian cancer experienced recurrences within a year or three, and that these recurrences most often killed them. I wore this specter like a lead cloak, and I felt sorry for myself most of the time. The thought of not seeing my children get older would strike me with such force that I'd find myself standing in the middle of the kitchen with my mouth hanging open, one hand clapped over it; the sight of either one of them peeling a tangerine or pulling on a sweater made my chest hurt. I spent so much time crying unexpectedly in public places that I invented a tear-wiping-away gesture: Press the first knuckles of both thumbs into your eye sockets—they fit in there perfectly and it actually feels good—and then just draw the knuckles across your eyes.

When it didn't hurt, or feel tragic, having a serious illness felt like a job, like the worst job in the world—hard, boring, and time-consuming beyond belief. I had to spend hours every day thinking about things I hated thinking about. My little investments and the wisdom of their "long-term" quality. Planning my next CAT scan or PET scan or checkup or blood test, and factoring in the three and a half hours that could allow that to happen: an hour at least to get across congested midtown Manhattan on the crosstown bus, an hour's time in the waiting room, twenty minutes in the examining room sitting in my paper smock on the crunchy examining-table paper waiting for the doctor to show up, and the hour-long return trip home on my throbbing legs.

I had a whole new career, a career of doing exactly the kinds of fussy things I was bad at. I had to meet with a lawyer about my will several times—at such a staggering hourly rate that I probably reduced my little "estate" by half. I had to submit claim forms to the insurance company every five minutes, resubmit them when the insurance company screwed up, write appeals when it tried to stiff me (one of my chemotherapy treatments was denied, while my thousand-dollar wig was covered in full). I had to remember to call for test results and remember to call to have the results faxed from one doctor to another before the next doctor's appointment, which I had to remember to make. (Chemo brain didn't help; I had the short-term memory of a rutabaga.) I had to sit on hold for so long when I called doctors' offices that by the time a human got on the line, I'd forgotten what I was calling about.

I have to stay alive, I told myself, because I have a husband and children.

I couldn't think of another reason.

It took a long time before it felt like there might be another point, one that included pleasure, or even fun.

But I started to have these moments here and there.

Two years after my treatments, my husband and I went to visit our daughter at camp in Maine. You can't believe how vast Maine is until you go there; you drive and you drive and you drive and you feel like you must have driven halfway to the north pole, and then you look at a map and you're still in the southern tip of the state, way down where it meets New Hampshire. It's distressing.

Anyway, we were driving back down to Massachusetts from the to-hell-and-gone camp, and after a couple of hours we were sick of driving and it was getting to be dinnertime, so we decided to stop in Freeport, one of the outlet-store capitals of the world. As soon as we stopped, we decided to stay, so we could just spend the evening going to the outlet stores, buying things.

First we had a nice, overpriced steak dinner in a restaurant in an old Victorian house, and then we bought five huge shopping bags' worth of clothes at J.Crew and Anne Klein. We ended up at L.L.Bean, the store that spawned all the other outlet stores in Freeport. L.L.Bean: the trustiest store on earth, the store that sells clothes with zippers that keep working long after their wearers have died, that replaces the item you're returning no questions asked, and practically before you return it.

L.L.Bean is the retail equivalent of coming home. Home is where they have to take you in, and so is L.L.Bean, where they are open 24 hours a day, 365 days a year. Why? Why bother? They could close one day a week; they could close at midnight. Nobody would get mad. The fact that they are always there, always open, is so impressive to me. People say, "I'm here for you," and sometimes it's true. I always know it's true with L.L.Bean.

For some reason, tonight we are the only customers at L.L.Bean. We wander among the displays of sturdy clothing made from twill and corduroy and flannel, of thick woolen blankets and indestructible canvas tote bags, greeted in every department by beaming senior-citizen salespeople: "We could monogram that for you right this minute if you like!"

In the furniture department we find two lemon-yellow Adirondack chairs. Their color suggests the sun of a summer day, their wide arms an invitation to rest a cool iced tea. While the friendly saleswoman goes off to figure out how quickly they can be shipped to us—and for free!—I sit down on a stack of area rugs and flip through a coffee-table book about Maine. One of the photographs is of a street in Stonington, a fishing village where my husband and older daughter and I used to go for a week every summer when she was a little girl. The picture is actually of the Stonington Opera House. It's a barny old building with OPERA HOUSE painted in fancy faded letters on the side. I remember taking a walk around town with my husband and daughter one Sunday morning, coming upon the building, and admiring the antique lettering and the aspirational quality of such a place in such a tiny town. I'm flooded with sadness that those days are gone, and with a longing for the young woman who had no idea she would ever get so sick. And I start to cry.

"Look," I say to my husband, who's standing nearby

looking uncomfortable; he doesn't know what to do when women cry in public places. "It's Stonington." He nods and mentions the names of a couple we know. After one of those aggravating Who's on First conversations, I realize that he thinks I'm talking about Stonington, Connecticut, another old seashore town, where we visited the couple once.

"You don't remember the Opera House?" I say. "We saw it on a walk?"

"No," he says helplessly. "It just didn't have the same impact on me."

I cry some more. The woman returns with the information, and I say, because I'm embarrassed about crying, "We used to go to the town in this picture, and I loved it."

"Oh," she says, smiling, as if women wept every day in her department, as if my tears gave her a welcome excuse to bring up a happy topic, "I feel that way about Campobello. I had so many summers there . . ."

Feeling understood, I wipe away my tears with my knuckle trick and ask her about Campobello. I'm not really listening; I'm still put out that my husband doesn't remember the Opera House, and I'm considering sulking seriously for the rest of the evening.

When we're finished shopping, we walk out into the parking lot through a side entrance. Even though we're in a parking lot, we're near thickets of trees, and there's that wonderful smell from the ground, that evening sigh—the earth, exhaling at the end of the day. And here, next to the entrance, is a gigantic boot. It's one of those L.L.Bean duck boots, with the ribbed rubber lower section and the leather upper—only this shoe is polyurethane, and it's as tall as a town house.

"You used to have boots like that," says my husband. I did. I wore them on snowy days when I first knew him in my twenties, and by then I'd already had them since high school.

He didn't remember the Opera House, but he remembers the boots. That's nice. Who could keep being mad?

We stand there and admire the shoe. The old woman who lived in a shoe could live in this shoe. It's as if Paul Bunyan had stomped through town and dropped his boot. Whose nutty idea was this huge boot?

How can you stay mad with two new lemon-yellow chairs coming to your house—knowing L.L.Bean, they will probably arrive there before you do—and picturing how great they are going to look on your lawn, near the weeping willow.

"Look at that," says my husband, pointing to a stand of tall pine trees on the other side of the parking lot. It's dark outside now. These trees are filled with colored lights, red and blue and green, the size of beach balls. They're like Christmas-tree ornaments, only much bigger, and it's not Christmas, it's July. They are just there to be cheerful, to perk up our parking-lot experience!

The moon is glowing, the giant ornaments are glowing, the big boot is glowing in the moonlight. And I think, How many times does a person get to be in a place that is both beautiful *and* ridiculous?

HAIR TODAY,
GONE TOMORROW

One night, after I'd started chemo for cancer but before the treatments had made my hair fall out, I ran into my friend Ruth. I'd met Ruth because she was my dentist—she was a gentle dentist, kind to those of us who showed up needing root canals because we'd neglected to floss in our twenties. "In terms of evolution," she'd say while we both waited for the laughing gas to get me stoned enough to let her in my mouth, "our teeth were only supposed to last us forty-five years, so you're doing great."

We'd become friends, which thrilled me; I was such a high-strung, pesky patient ("You say the nitrous is at its 'legal limit,' but, you know, if you turn it up a smidge, no one's going to *report* you"), I couldn't imagine she'd want to spend a minute more with me than she had to. Now our kids went to the same high school, in large part because she'd recommended the school. And by awful coincidence, we both had the same kind of cancer—only Ruth was much farther down the chemo path than I was and had already lost her hair.

I'd seen her a few weeks earlier and she'd been wearing a scarf, but when I ran into her at a school play, here it was, her old corona of curly hair.

"Ruth, your hair looks so great!" I said.

"It's a wig! I never thought I'd wear a wig, but sometimes it's nice when you go out. It feels dressy. A little creepy, but dressy."

When I looked at the wig more closely, I could tell it was a wig, but barely. Her wig hair was a little glossier than her real hair, but that was it. And if Ruth felt good in a wig, maybe I would too. It seemed unlikely, but possible.

"You should get one, Jenny," she said. "Medical insurance covers the whole thing." This seemed so bizarre as to be unbelievable, but she insisted it was true.

I've never thought of my hair as one of my strong suits. I've always thought it was one of my weaker suits—maybe, appearance-wise, my weakest. I grew up in the sixties and seventies, when you were supposed to have absolutely straight, long hair, as smooth as a plank of polished wood, even if you had to scorch it with your mother's iron to get it that way. Invariably parted down the middle, the ideal hair fell in great lank sheets to your waist. More than one girl at my high school had hair so long they would smooth it down, carefully, and sit on it, like a bridal train.

My hair was, mortifyingly, a thick, springy, unwieldy

mass. On top, it looked like straw, like a thatched roof; on the sides and around my neck, crazy ringlets and curlicues coiled this way and that. When I'd try to grow it out, it never got longer; it grew sideways, like a mushroom cap or a sphinx's headdress. Kids called me Brillo and Medusa, and I suffered mightily. I'd sit in class and watch, dying a little, as the straight-haired girls tossed their silky manes over their shoulders, languidly ran their fingers through them, held up a horse tail's worth to examine, like scientists at a microscope, their split ends.

As an adult I've done the best I could with my hair, given that I can't stand sitting in beauty salons for the hours it would take to do anything ambitious to it. Occasionally I get it blow-dried, and it looks good, I have to say. People barely recognize me; then, when they do, they pay me compliments.

"You should wear it that way all the time!" they say.

"I'll do that!"

Three or five days later it's reverted to an old coarse thicket again, people stop saying things, and I forget what I said about wearing my hair that way all the time. After a lifetime of disappointment, I feel about my hair the way people who've been divorced for a long time think about their spouses—I have to deal with it once in a while (get it cut and, in recent years, colored), and I'm pleasantly surprised when it behaves well, but I'm not exactly holding my breath.

So when I got cancer, I wasn't that upset about losing my hair. When I thought about it at all, I hoped that having cancer might *improve* my hair. I'd heard stories about women whose hair had grown back in an entirely new version—livelier where it had been limp, or loose waves replacing a frizzy tangle. These women had a whole second life—a second, successful marriage!—to better hair.

But no matter how you feel about losing your hair, the prospect of not having any forces you to make decisions that seem, uncomfortably, to go to the heart of who you are. Losing your hair becomes less about losing your hair than about other things. What kind of cancer person was I going to be?

I knew I didn't want to go around bald. This seemed too in-your-face and, frankly, a little show-offy: *I have cancer, deal with it.*

A scarf or a wig, those were my choices. (This was a few years ago; these days, I've read, you can get "cold caps" to wear during chemo treatments; they constrict the blood vessels in your scalp, protecting your hair follicles from the effects of the chemo. They're only effective about 50 to 60 percent of the time, but I'd probably try it anyway. Why not?)

The scarf person, it seemed to me, knows that any person with a brain will guess why she's suddenly wearing a scarf all the time. The wig person, on the other hand, hopes that even the people who can tell she's wearing a wig will assume she's wearing it because she doesn't want to talk about why. The wig person is saying, to herself and to others, "Please, God, just let me blend in."

I totally understood that feeling. I did. I was already getting stopped on the street by people I didn't know that well, people who'd been told I had cancer; they'd grip my arm and say, with an intimacy I didn't think they'd earned,

"How *are* you?" It felt invasive. I couldn't help it: I'd take a step back and say, "*Good*, how are *you*?"

But I decided that my "truer" self would wear a scarf. Wearing a wig seemed to be going out of the way to kowtow to some outmoded notion that you had to hide your cancer, keep it hush-hush. I wasn't ashamed of having cancer, dammit! I would go out into the world in my forthright scarves and bandannas, and to hell with discretion.

My little encounter with Ruth and her wig had opened up another possibility. I was being too rigid, too black-and-white, about this wig-versus-scarf thing. I could wear a wig sometimes, and other times not. A wig might be fun as a change of pace. And it was free. And I love free things, particularly when my insurance company pays for them. What was the harm?

I bought my wig at a wig store near Columbus Circle, settling on a nice light brown one, made from human, not synthetic, hair that matched my own hair color. The wig fitter fussed with it forever, but when he was finally done, I thought I looked surprisingly okay, meaning that my wig didn't look too wiggy. It had soft bangs that cleverly obscured that unfortunate forehead area where you can usually see the edge of the wig, and the hair fell in nice, natural-looking layers. It looked much better than my real hair, which pleased me.

A few weeks went by between my buying the wig and my hair falling out. When you have chemo, your hair doesn't fall out all at once. It gives up the ghost gradually, first in strands, and then in little clumps that you notice in the shower drain that make you think there's a dead mouse down there.

Every time you look in the mirror, your baldness reminds you that you're very sick, in spite of all the cheerfulness and optimism you've talked yourself into. And you're not *completely* bald; random wisps of hair still cling to your head, and that makes it worse somehow.

But I wasn't ready for the wig yet. I looked at it a lot, on its white Styrofoam wig head on top of the radiator cover in my bedroom, but the wig head intimidated me—it managed, even without a face, to seem haughty—and the wig seemed to belong to her more than me.

I wore my scarves instead. People guessed that I had cancer and asked how I was feeling. "I'm good!" I kept saying, and the more I said it, the less I believed it, which made me say it even more brightly. "I'm great! Doing *great*!" All this faux cheer made me feel like the coach of a team that wasn't doing that great, especially when people looked at me as if they were about to cry. I didn't blame them— well, I did blame them, but I shouldn't have.

I wearied of the questions, and I wearied of my look, my daily uniform of scarves and bandannas. I felt like a lady pirate, or one of those eighty-seven-year-old women wheeling their grocery carts down Broadway. Then my eyebrows fell out. For some reason, I didn't expect this at all, and felt surprisingly sorry for myself. My hair was part of my head, I thought, but my eyebrows were part of my *face*. I felt exposed, and vulnerable. I now looked like a big bald baby.

Every time I looked in the mirror and saw the baby, I felt so bad for her I wanted to cry.

I needed a buffer between my head and the world. I needed people to stop looking at me and asking how I was feeling. I was ready for my wig.

My friend Martha's daughter Anna was graduating from the University of Chicago, and I'd flown out for the weekend. This seemed like the perfect, grown-up, festive occasion to inaugurate my wig.

The morning of the graduation, I put on my wig—this takes much longer than it sounds, with a lot of fussing at stray strands of your own hair and brushing of your wig hair—and start walking toward the campus, surrounded by the throngs of graduating seniors' families.

I feel weird walking along in my wig out in public. I feel like an impostor. As if I've just done something illegal, robbed a bank maybe, and am now trying to blend in with the crowd by going incognito in my wig. I'm startled every time I see myself reflected in a store window—it's my face, but in someone else's hair. I keep pulling and poking at my wig, trying to adjust it, fretting that my scalp is exposed.

I get to the huge main quad of the campus, set up with an ocean of white folding chairs for the ceremony. The weather report says it's 97 degrees in Chicago, but it feels like a good 115, and it's only ten in the morning.

Then, in the crowd, I see Eden, an editor of mine from New York, and remember that her son is graduating today too. Eden is a terrific editor, and a kind one—instead of saying, "This piece is *way* too long," she'll say, "This lovely piece is going to be so hard to cut!"

She is also famously well organized. "Here, Jenny! Take one of these!" she says, holding out the several wide-brimmed sun hats that she's brought along in case she runs into some dimwit who hasn't put it together that we'll be sitting under the scalding Chicago sun for several hours.

I thank her, take one of the hats, and put it on, but only partly so I won't get sunburned. Mostly because I won't feel as self-conscious in a hat. I want my wig under wraps.

The procession takes forever. Hundreds of sweltering students walk down the outdoor aisle in their caps and gowns, smiling gamely for their parents, while grandparents fan themselves with their programs. The ceremony takes even longer. By the second hour or so, my head is baking—no, broiling. Lines of sweat roll down from under my wig onto my neck. The wig feels heavier and hotter by the minute; I feel like I'm wearing my cat on my head.

If I take off the hat, I think desperately, maybe a little air will get through the wig and onto my head. I take off the hat. For a split second, I think, Whew! This is so much better! All that hot weight is gone!

Wait. There's something in my hat, which I am now holding in my hand.

My wig. My wig is in my hat. So what's on my head?

Years ago, when my sister and I discovered that her station wagon was missing from its parking space outside my apartment building—stolen, it turned out—we both stood on the sidewalk staring at the space, as if the car would somehow materialize. Now I do the equivalent: I touch my palm to the top of my head, as if there might be another wig up there. Nope.

This is so surprising, so beyond embarrassing, that it's impossible to be embarrassed, because embarrassment can't even begin to cover it. I have lost everything—my hat, my wig, my hair, my health—and I feel strangely . . . free. I laugh, because it's funny—having gone to all this trouble only to end up like this, like Lucille Ball. *Rickeeee!*

I jam the wig and the hat back on my head. Not for me, I'm way past that, but for the people behind me. I can't even imagine their expressions. I feel awful for having shocked them.

When I get home, I put the wig in the back of my top dresser drawer, wrapped in a plastic bag, and I stick to wearing scarves. After my chemo is done, my hair grows back—it's the same old wacky hair, but for the first time in my life I'm glad to see it. My wig stays in the drawer for the next three years. Every time I see it I think, My God! What's a pelt doing in here? But I keep the wig because it was expensive, and I can't imagine throwing away anything so expensive, even if I didn't pay for it.

Ruth's hair grows back too, and for the next two years we do normal things together—worry about our children, eat the delicious pot roast she cooks at her house, tell stories about having cancer. She loves my wig story, and she does the best rendition of something that happens a lot when you have ovarian cancer: People tell you an inspiring story about their mother or aunt and how she had ovarian cancer too, and how, once it went into remission, she got her Ph.D. or took up parasailing and had a whole new life.

"How's she doing?" you ask the teller of the story.

"Oh. She died," they say, looking stricken.

"Do it again, Ruth!" I say when she and I are together. "Do the inspiring people!" We crack each other up with our stories.

Then Ruth has a recurrence of her cancer that goes on for two years, and finally she dies. I miss her so much. And Eden, my editor—who didn't know she had cancer at the graduation—dies too. In light of these losses, tossing away my wig seems way too cocky. Who am I to say that I'm done with being sick, that I might not have some occasion—something fancy, on a cooler day—when I'll want to wear it again?

One day I read one of those bossy magazine articles about decluttering your closet. Ask yourself, realistically, if you are ever going to wear that old piqué bridesmaid's dress or pair of culottes ever again, the article instructs. If the answer is no, throw them out.

I think, Realistically? Realistically I might be needing those chemo drugs again, and I might lose my hair again. But I will never, ever wear that stupid wig again. Better to wear the stupid scarves and get stared at and have people look at me as if they're about to cry. Better to let the other women out there walking around with no hair see that I'm one of them.

So I threw it away.

I HAVE TO GO NOW

I'm sorry! I'm sorry! I didn't mean to close the cupboard that hard! I hope I didn't wake you up!

I'm just looking for the coffee filters. It was so sweet of you last night to say, "If you're up before us, just help yourself to whatever. The coffee is pretty self-explanatory."

I'm sorry, I apologize, please forgive me—and thank you again for inviting me!—but doesn't *self-explanatory* mean "self-explanatory," like it shouldn't need an explanation? Like I should be able to just come in here and find the things I need to make coffee all together, and within a few minutes gurgling coffee-making sounds and that exciting coffee smell would start coming out of the coffeemaker?

It took me a long time to even find the coffeemaker. It didn't look like a coffeemaker. It looked like a rocket ship. I kept passing it by on my tours of the counters, thinking it was—I don't know, I didn't think about it too much, but something complicated: a crème-fraîche-culture incubator, maybe; a sorbet churner; a homemade-bialy steamer-cooker thing.

Please forgive me, a thousand forgive me's, if I seem to be rude, but the rocket-ship machine didn't say "coffeemaker" to me, it didn't cry out, "Here I am, groggy friend, brave traveler, you who have come to this country place far from your city home, anxious about the burdens of being a houseguest, not the least of which is having to stumble around a kitchen that is not your kitchen. Together we will make a cup of cheering, flavorful hot coffee to help you begin your day."

I only know this machine is the coffeemaker because I've found this little basket in it that swings out—you have to press a hidden button to get it to pop out, like a secret tunnel behind a bookcase, something designed by Nancy Drew or (it's German, I see by the annoying umlauts over the vowels in the brand name on the side) Stasi officers. The basket is shaped like a wide cone, and it looks like a filter should fit in there. Let us hope.

So where are the filters? I have been opening and closing cupboards for many minutes, minutes in which I have felt, unaccountably, somehow stealthy, like a prowler; and at the same time guilty, like I've come here under the guise of guest but I am really here to probe into your personal life. And you think I am your friend! I'm so worried—terrified, really—that you two might come downstairs and think I'm looking for something secret, trying to find something here in the kitchen that you stashed away because you're embarrassed by it. I can't even imagine what that would be (A cigarette from 1983? An old bong?), but that's how I feel.

I haven't found anything naughty—I don't want to,

believe me!—but I do feel that I've intruded on your personal life in a way that makes me feel ashamed. I'm sorry I discovered the Metamucil section, and the cans of Ensure.

Forgive me, but I thought the filters might be in the same vicinity as the coffeemaker. Some people find that helpful. On the counter next to the coffeemaker, for example, or in the cupboard right above it. It's just a suggestion.

I have an idea. I am going to Turn It Over about the coffee filters. I am going to put them into the hands of my Higher Filter Power, and I am going to look for the coffee instead. Maybe, while I am looking for the coffee, the filters will show up. Near the coffee. That seems unlikely. Just kidding, mostly!

In our house we keep the coffee in the freezer. That keeps it fresh. In your house, I see, you do not. In your house, in your freezer, you keep—oh, crap! landslide!—several huge old bags of ice you got for a long-ago party that are now frozen into big blocks, and half-used boxes of Birds Eye green beans and a smashed ancient Eskimo Pie. I've managed to catch everything in my arms, avoiding a noisy clatter onto the floor, and I'll just stick it all back now, in a way that will prevent another avalanche. It's a good idea, I've found, to arrange heavy things, like ten-pound blocks of ice, underneath lighter objects, like crushed Eskimo Pies.

Oh, look, here's a closet, a closet with shelves full of paper towels and laundry detergent. And here in the closet is a can of coffee! A can of Café Du Monde coffee from New Orleans! Wonderful news! But—maybe it's not your "real" coffee, the coffee you use every day. It's sort of in the wrong location, in this closet near the back door, away from the more active part of the kitchen, and it's unopened. Maybe it's for a special occasion—maybe it's for an annual at-home Mardi Gras celebration, maybe you got it on a romantic trip to New Orleans and are saving it for your anniversary. Is it all right to open this, or not? Would that make me a bad person?

A moot point, I guess, since there are no filters in here anyway.

I want to go home. May I go home now? It's not you, it really isn't. I'm sorry I'm so snippy. Who am I to be snippy about anything? My own freezer is so frightening, so full of old chocolate Easter eggs and unloved Mary Janes from Halloweens past, that I don't even like to look in there; Jeffrey Dahmer could have stored a head or a tibia in the back of it for all I know.

I'm just uncomfortable here. I'm uncomfortable not in my own home. I'm uncomfortable in my own home also, but that's not what I'm trying to say.

I'm trying to say that I just don't think I can do this— this being a weekend guest, this protracted socializing. It's a strain on me. You think I'm devil-may-care and chatty and entertaining enough for an entire weekend, but truly, I am not. I am just not up to this.

What are we going to do after breakfast? Go into town and shop? Where is town? Is there coffee there? I could go there now and get some coffee, a nice hot paper cup of it, just to tide me over.

Am I allowed to take your car? I have no idea. I don't know if I would return from town to have you say, "Of course it's all right to take the car, don't be silly!" or to find you sitting at the kitchen table trying to smile but hurt, surprised by my presumption. "No, no, it's fine, did you have a good time?" you might say, and I could tell it wasn't fine at all.

After we go shopping or whatever, are we going to be having lunch? I don't like to admit it, but I'm not one of those people who say, "I had a big breakfast"—are we going to have breakfast, by the way? I'm starving, but you seem to be sleeping in, you seem to have been sleeping, like newborns, for something like fourteen hours, I never know how people do that, like it's a sport!—"I had a big breakfast so I'll just grab a snack for lunch." I never just grab a snack for lunch. I like to have a big breakfast and a big lunch and a big dinner. But I can't figure out how to say that to you in so many words.

What I'll do is offer to take you out for lunch. That way I know I'll get in a square meal before dinner. I hope it doesn't cost that much, though, because I'm already taking you out for dinner, as we discussed. I feel poor already.

Did someone say something last night about playing bridge today if it rained? I seem to remember the husband in that nice couple who came for dinner suggesting it—it touched me how you could tell that even though he was talking about playing bridge as if he thought it were a campy idea, something our parents might do, he really wanted to do it. And did I say something like "Oh, I don't know how to play bridge, but I'd love to learn!" If I did, that's because I felt sorry for him. Also, I think I was kind of drunk at the time.

I would not love to learn. I would hate to learn. Bridge is unlearnable by me. You have to have a partner and strategy and write things down on little pads of paper and somehow store in your memory the previous moves of others, like a squirrel storing nuts, for use later. It sounds like a job. A job I would get fired from on the first day, before lunch.

I can't do strategy. I can't think four moves down the line. I can't think one move down the line. Three-year-olds cream me at checkers. Some people know how to beat the lights walking in the city—"Come on come on come on!" they say, knowing that if you miss this light, you'll have to stand at the next seventeen street corners. I hate that way of getting around town. I feel like I'm in some kind of race. I'd rather stand at an intersection like a bump on a log. I wait for the light to say WALK, then I walk across the street and down the sidewalk and hang around at the next corner until the next light says WALK, then I cross that street and go down that sidewalk and wait at that corner until that light says WALK. It takes me about two hours to walk twenty blocks. I don't care. It's all my brain can handle. And sometimes while I stand there, I remember a funny joke someone told me last Tuesday, and I crack up.

Anyway, I can't do games of skill, only chance. Games with dice. I like dice. You rolls 'em and you takes your chances!

I like moving my guy around the board; it's pleasant. My guy or my little Hershey's Kiss–shaped plastic piece; I try to get a green one because green is my favorite color. But I don't mind if green is your favorite color too—you can have the green, I'll take the color no one else wants, usually orange. I don't care. I'm not very competitive, as you can tell.

What I like best are games of chance where there is also a story. For example, Parcheesi has no story—you're just going around that board—so I don't like it that much. I like Clue—I like those tiny weapons! I like Chutes and Ladders. Chutes and Ladders isn't much of a story—you ascend, you backslide, you ascend again, you backslide some more—but it has a visceral appeal to me. It feels exactly like every day of life itself.

I like the game called the Game of Life. The story of the Game of Life is a not-imaginative, even morally corrupt one—the point seems to be mostly to make money and buy things and end your days, if you're lucky, living in Millionaire Estates—but it's a story. It has tension and uncertainty, even if the uncertainty is about whether you are going to get a mortgage. Speaking of real estate, I like Monopoly—now, there's a game with hardly any skill involved; you only have to know what every Manhattan toddler knows: Buy, don't rent.

You don't have an old Candy Land lying around, do you? Candy Land is the best game ever. Candy Land is a true quest, an odyssey. Candy Land has everything: exotic locales (e.g., the Lollipop Woods), peril (the looming threat of getting stuck in the Molasses Swamp), brushes with royalty (the cruel Lord Licorice, the lovely Queen Frostine) and, of course, candy. What more could a person want?

I'm also worried that, after our games-playing, we may run out of things to talk about at dinner tonight. If we do, I can tell a story. I have three stories: the time I met Philip Roth and he was mean to me, the time our cat ate our hamster, and the time I thought I had ESP for a month. Altogether, they take about forty minutes to tell, so I hope you will interrupt me a lot. Otherwise I will have run out of things to say and it will only be eight-thirty.

I guess I don't have to tell you my feelings about the crossword puzzle, if you're planning on doing that on Sunday morning. What's a seventeen- or twenty-three-letter word for "I can't do that either"? A baboon could do better. But even if I could do it, I just can't see the point. People always say doing the crossword keeps your brain sharp, but it seems only to keep your brain sharp in the parallel reality of crossword-puzzle land, a land in which EHumperdinck is still a star and it actually matters that you know that Yale's motto is *Lux et veritas*. And I'm sorry, I don't like it when people sit there in front of you and do the puzzle in pen. I don't care how sharp you feel; I'd enjoy your company more if you were lying in a pool of your own senile drool.

So I'm a little worried about Sunday as well.

Maybe I should just take my meals in my room until it's time to go home. You could leave them on a tray outside my bedroom door.

Speaking of leaving, do you want me to strip the bed before I go? Maybe I'll fashion a rope out of the sheets, like in the movies, and depart out of my bedroom window, quietly.

No time like the present.

Please forgive me. This is just too hard. Thank you very much for having me. I'm sorry. I really am.

THE TROUBLE WITH NATURE

A lot of people who live in the city like to visit the country to get close to nature. Then, once they are in the country, they find that they needn't go outdoors to get close to nature. Nature comes right inside, as if to prove some kind of point.

Often it is nickel-sized gray spiders, weaving their webs in the upper corners of several rooms, or crawling up and down the walls to start a new web in another corner. Some people get a paper towel and clear away the webs and the spiders, but many people worry that the spiders will fall onto their bodies and so leave the webs and the spiders alone, avoiding corners of rooms altogether.

Or sometimes a black thing has attached itself to the kitchen ceiling. It is the exact size and shape of a charcoal briquette, and you wonder what a charcoal briquette is doing up there. On closer inspection, it turns out to be a bat, hanging upside down. As if the kitchen ceiling, so close you can press your palm against it, were the vaulted recesses of a cathedral, or the dark rafters of an old barn.

Its little body is covered in fur, which many people find distressing. This is a creature that flies, and it is as unsettling for a flying thing to have fur as it would be for a hard-boiled egg, or a rose petal, to have it. Distressing too are its pointed ears, which are sticking straight up—down, actually—and are shaped just like a Chihuahua's ears, only in miniature. Perfect tiny doggy ears, which also do not belong on a flying thing. And the black briquette body and the pointy upside-down ears form a silhouette that instantly sears itself into many people's memory bank of disturbing images. They know that decades from now, when they are old and remember nothing—not their name, not the pabulum the nurse's aide spooned into their mouth moments earlier—they will remember that silhouette. They may die with that silhouette, not their loved ones, as the last image playing in their broken old brains.

Some people shoo the bats out the door with a section of the newspaper. Other people try to go about their day and not look at the bat, leaving the kitchen door propped wide open in the hope that the bat will eventually fly out on its own. These people would just rather not see the bat's wings. At the moment, the wings are folded flat against the bat's body while it hangs there. But sooner or later the bat will fly away, and in spite of themselves people often get a glimpse of the wings. They look like they are made out of paper-thin black leather—another distressing detail, like the fur. Also, the wings are webbed, like a duck's feet, which makes some people feel like they might vomit.

Unlike bats, the small birds that fly indoors by accident

hardly ever find their way back outside on their own; they just keep whacking into plate-glass windows and walls and table lamps, unable to locate the tear in the porch screen or the open window they flew in through two minutes earlier. This futile flinging of themselves, at once heartbreaking and irksome, drives many people to get a broom and try to shoo the bird back in the direction of the tear in the porch screen or the open window.

Except the bird still doesn't get it, and many people finally give up and go to bed while the bird is still banging around, and sometimes they find its corpse on the floor in the morning, close to the torn screen, where it expired—bravely, birdbrainedly—just before finding its way to freedom. Many people can feel the weight and shape of the bird's stiff little corpse through the paper towel they wrap it in to throw it away and feel confused—at once mournful, guilty, and deeply repulsed.

Repellent also is something happening on the kitchen counters. One day the butter plate gets left on the counter by mistake, and when you return to the kitchen two minutes later, the stick of butter on the plate is covered with a million tiny ants—not those big black ones; these are reddish, much smaller, and faster, even manic—like a crawling carpet. It's like a scene from *The Lost Weekend*, or something in a Salvador Dalí painting. After the butter incident the ant attacks keep happening, day after day, swarms of them laying siege to a drop of maple syrup, or a bit of apple peel that has fallen onto the counter. Many people run out and buy those small containers of ant poison and set them about on the counters, but that is a waste of time, as the ants swarm up, over, and past them like fleet-footed marathon runners.

People usually don't see the mice. They just see their tiny black droppings in the morning, also on the kitchen counters. Even the most sophisticated mousetraps are a waste of money, for the mice know to avoid them. Between the mice doo-doo and the ants, many people feel that the kitchen counters are a health hazard and long to take their meals elsewhere, at restaurants, except that the only restaurants are miles away.

Some people think raccoons are cute, but this is only because they have never seen one rooting through the "tamper-proof" trash cans in the garage. Raccoon paws are attenuated and thin, more like human fingers, with long, tapered, manicured-looking nails, like the too-long nails of the bank teller who counted out your cash yesterday. Many people find that the human-looking paws make them want to vomit again. Nonetheless, they try bringing a radio into the garage and blasting loud music at the raccoons, which the Internet says will scare them away, but doesn't.

At this juncture, many people take themselves upstairs to their bedroom and lie down and stare at the ceiling, hoping that if they focus all of their thoughts and "energy" on the raccoons going away, maybe, maybe this will happen. While they are staring at the ceiling, they notice that the spiderwebs now have something suspended in them—small brown balls the size of baby peas. These, they realize, are egg sacs, filled with thousands upon thousands of tiny spiders yet to be born.

Some people are able to not dwell on the egg sacs and the thought of what is shortly to come out of them. But many people cannot help thinking about it. They begin to consider living in the out-of-doors, where creatures keep to themselves, in a bush or up a tree, and mostly out of sight— Mother Nature at her most sublime.

SPEAK, MEMORY

You know what I'm tired of? People being so down on themselves for not remembering things. Doesn't it seem like everyone you know over a certain age is spending way too much time saying, "Dammit, I just saw that movie yesterday, and I can't remember what it's called. This is terrible." That's so negative. Quitcherbellyachin'! Celebrate what you do remember!

For example, I was in Duane Reade the other day, forgetting what I was there for and, yes, getting bummed out about that. Then I remembered that I was there for some kind of hair product, only I couldn't remember what it was. Then I remembered that it was the stuff you wash your hair with that comes in a bottle, but I couldn't remember what they call it, so I knew I wouldn't be able to ask any of the employees to help me find it. Just as I was about to throw myself a great big pity party there in the hair-care aisle, my eye caught a display of those fake-tortoiseshell headbands. And my brain said, "Lynne Tryforos."

What the—?! I thought. And then I decided to turn things around—to just enjoy the moment, to take pleasure in the workings of my brain. I had a fun time right there in Duane Reade—it was like playing a game—trying to put together why this name had popped into my head. It came to me: Lynne Tryforos was the secretary and girlfriend of the Scarsdale Diet doctor, and the reason that Jean Harris, who was also his girlfriend and had preceded Lynne Tryforos, shot him—and Jean Harris wore that same kind of headband!

I think it's so neat that my brain remembered that. Why did it, when the names of so many people I actually know, and sometimes my own phone number, are lost to me? Who can say? The brain is a mystery, a wonderful, labyrinthine mystery.

I say let's put these random bits of information to use, to help us. For instance, when the conversation turns to Jean Harris and the Scarsdale Diet doctor, and somebody asks, "Why did she shoot him again?" and you pipe up, "Lynne Tryforos," people who have just met you will think you remember other things as well, lots of other things, when in fact you could not tell them what you had for breakfast. They'll think you're smart, which is great, since you never know these days when you'll be fired from your job and you might need one of these people to recommend you for a new one. They don't need to know that with your antique, outmoded "skill set," you would be lucky to find employment as a lunchroom lady.

Granted, the whole Scarsdale Diet–doctor thing doesn't come up in conversation too often. You will just have to cleverly steer it in that direction, like so:

You: *Headmistress*. Now that's a word you don't hear too much anymore.

Other Person: That is so true!

You: I think the last time I heard it was in reference to Jean Harris.

Other Person: Jean Harris. Was she the lady who shot the diet doctor?

You: Exactly. Because he was having an affair with his secretary, Lynne Tryforos.

Other Person: Get out of town! Good God, how do you remember that? You're amazing!

You: I don't know about that, but I do seem to be re-membering *more* things as I get older. I feel sharper than ever, and totally up for new challenges. In fact, if you hear of any jobs, maybe you'd suggest me.

Other Person: That I will!

Also, once we stop thinking of these "meaningless" bits of information that come to us out of the blue as annoying and disconcerting, we can start having fun with them, fold-ing them into our social discourse like frothy egg whites:

You: Don't you remember the strangest things some-times?

Other Person: I'll say. The other day I was thinking about my fifth-grade teacher, Hyla Jones, and how strange it was that I remembered her first name when I don't remem-ber the first names of the many dozens of other teachers I had over the years. I mean, Hyla is an unusual name, but really, I'm sure some of my other teachers had unusual names.

You: That's so fascinating! Speaking of elementary school, the other day I remembered the lunch box my friend Dana Cole had in the third grade. It was shaped like a school bus, and it had all the Disney characters waving out of the windows of the bus. Before I saw hers, I really liked my lunch box, which was plaid, but after I saw hers, I just wanted hers.

Other Person: That's such a compelling story. Poignant, even.

You: You know what else I remember? Almost the entire cast of *Where the Boys Are*: Dolores Hart; George Hamilton; Frank Gorshin—in a pair of funny glasses!; Jim Hutton; Connie Francis, who also sang the title song; Yvette Mimieux; and Paula Prentiss.

Other Person: Outstanding! I forgot about Dolores Hart. I thought that was Mitzi Gaynor.

You: Mitzi Gaynor?!? No way! She was in *South Pacific*.

Other Person: Of course! I remember all the words to "I'm Gonna Wash That Man Right Outa My Hair."

You: Me too!

Other Person: Let's sing it right now!

You: And let's do the same moves she did—let's act like we're in the shower, doing whaddyacallit to our hair.

Other Person: Shampooing it?

You: *Shampooing!* Yes! Oh, thank you!

Other Person: Say, do you ever find it sad that now our memories are made up of a few odd, insignificant bits stuck there like chewed-up gum to the underside of a classroom desk, and that come to us unbidden and out of nowhere, but that if you try to remember something important, like how to do long division, you cannot?

You: Not at all! We should take pleasure in what comes to us while we are sitting there not remembering math. Like, Mike Nesmith's mother invented Liquid Paper. Once I ate spaghetti and meatballs at my friend Anne Dumke's house, and once I peed in the woods with my neighbor Carl Walsh. Barbie's nerdy friend in the Barbie board game was named Poindexter. Terry Southern's coauthor on *Candy* was named Mason Hoffenberg. I could go on and on.

CAN I HAVE YOUR ERRANDS?

Hello, Errand Lady. I don't know your name, but I just found your list of errands in the supermarket, at the bottom of my grocery cart. Here is your list, written on the back of a marked-up scorecard that says Misty Meadows Golf & Tennis Club:

> Take in Lexus
> Derm—filler
> Take R to groomer
> B Bros—suspenders
> Gin, vodka

I love your handwriting. I always wanted to have handwriting like yours, pleasingly rounded, with lots of loops—the *l*'s are shaped like ovals standing on end—and with those *n*'s that look like *u*'s and *m*'s that look like *w*'s. It's the handwriting of boarding-school girls, girls who never failed to write their thank-you notes:

Dear Graudwa,

Thauk you so wuch for geuerously coveriug wy tuitiou to Wiss Porter's. So far I aw loviug every wi-uute. My classes are very stiwulatiug. My roowwate Casey is really great. She is frow Uew Cauaau.

Thauk you agaiu, aud Wuch Love, Uaucy

If I had the same lovely handwriting as you, maybe I would have the same errands as you. That's kind of true, when you think about it. I mean, if I had that same handwriting, it would be because I had grown up in that kind of milieu, one that would probably have led to a life a lot more like yours than mine, which I would love.

My errands blow, they really do. Here's my list. You don't even have to read past *Laundromat* to get the idea— *Laundromat* kind of says it all, doesn't it?—but here goes:

Laundromat
Dump
Hardware store: termite killer stuff, Drano,
duct tape for lamp cord & dishwasher & pipes
Plastic for windows
Find job!!!

See what I mean? I don't want to sound bitter—I'm not, honest—but have you ever even written the word *Laundro-mat*? I didn't think so. Anyway, it wouldn't look like a word if you wrote it. It would look like *Lauudrowat*.

I have this idea: Let me do your errands for you—just for a day. It would make me the happiest girl in the world.

Okay, first I will take in the Lexus. I assume this means that I am taking it to your Lexus dealer because there's something wrong with it. Nothing hugely wrong, because it's a Lexus, after all, and it's pretty new—just, like, the image on that TV screen on the dashboard that shows whether you're about to back into a tree or whatnot is a little too fuzzy for your liking. If you have a Lexus, you shouldn't have to put up with that sort of thing, right?

The exciting thing about taking the Lexus to the dealership is that they are going to give me a loaner while they repair your car. That's what they do if you have an expensive car—they give you another Lexus while they fix yours. I won't mind. *Au contraire!* I will love it! "Oh, this one's just a loaner," I will say to people. God, I want to be able to say that so bad.

Next I will go to the Derm—that's your dermatologist, of course—and get filler, to plump up the wrinkles in my face. Oh, boy! Normally I object to this sort of thing, but I am going to give myself a pass for the day. I'll release myself from the burden of my prissy self-righteous objections about caving in to our culture's obsession with youth and appearance blah blah blah. To tell you the truth, that will be a big relief. Because these wrinkles are just a total bummer, and anything I've said about not minding them, or wearing them with pride, is utter bullshit.

So after I get my face all rejuvenated, I will take R to the groomer. I bet R is your dog. I bet he is a bichon frise, or a labradoodle. He was probably supposed to be your children's dog, but they're always forgetting to walk and feed him, and anyway, it's you who spends the day with him while they're at school, so he's more your dog now. You complain about that, but you adore R.

I'm not really a dog person, I have to say, so I hope it is all right if I make R sit in the back of the car. You probably let him sit in the passenger seat, but I don't want him putting his head in my lap and slobbering all over me. But you know what I will love about R? Just having the kind of life, if only for a day, in which taking a dog to the groomer is a thing, an important thing, I have to do. "Did you have a good day?" your husband probably says to you when he gets home from work, and some days you say, "Well, I took Rusty to the groomer," and he says, "Oh, thanks! He sure needed it. I'm so glad you don't have a job so that you have the time to get these things done." And you say, "I know, right?!"

Speaking of your husband, I guess he's the one I'm picking up the suspenders at Brooks Brothers for. The only guys I know who wear suspenders are money guys, and I'm probably not going too far out on a limb here when I say I'm thinking that your husband is most likely an investment banker of some sort. I've never understood the message that investment bankers are trying to send with suspenders— "I'm the sort of fellow whose pants will never fall down, so you can trust me with your money"?—but never mind, never mind. Whatever makes him feel good about himself is important, and I will feel good knowing that I have done my part in making him so ridiculously successful.

I'm almost done with your errands, but first I have to stop at the liquor store. Are you having a party? Is that what the gin and vodka are for? Good for you. You could invite me if you want. You know what kind of friends I bet you have? The kind who drink all the time but don't know they're alcoholics. They don't even secretly suspect it—they're just totally clueless, the way people used to be in the fifties. Amazing that such people still exist, but they do. People who still say, "It must be five o'clock somewhere!" and start hoisting Bloody Marys—glug glug glug!—at 10:00 a.m. on a Saturday.

I hope your friends are like that because these are the kind of people who are a lot of fun to drink with. They never say to you, "Are you sure you haven't had enough?" They don't even ask you if you want another drink—they just keep bringing you fresh drinks, over and over. Of course you want more, they think; you're there, aren't you?

So after I get the alcohol, I'm done. But just before I deliver the loaner Lexus and R and the booze and the suspenders to you, I'll take a few minutes. I'll park somewhere for a little while and just sit and breathe in the fabulous smell of that leather interior, and flip through the copy of *Town & Country* I found next to your seat, and think, What a great, great day.

HOW TO TAKE DAD
TO THE DOCTOR

With Dad, your adventure is sure to begin even before it starts.

You pick him up at his retirement-community condo. It's your job to drive Dad places, as he has had his license revoked for nearly mowing down all the students in the local Montessori preschool and their teacher. In Dad's version, he confused the gas pedal with the brake because the children "were distracting me."

As you pull out of the driveway, Dad will pretend not to hear the loud, insistent beep-beep-beep signaling that someone doesn't have his seat belt on. You bring the car to a stop.

"What is it now?" Dad says, as if this were the last in a string of calamities that have happened on your expedition, though it is only 8:15 a.m. and you arrived at his condo three minutes ago and absolutely nothing has happened yet.

In the interest of getting him to the doctor in a timely

manner, you have made a point of not commenting on the opened package of mint Milanos on his kitchen counter or the crumbs around his mouth indicating that he has once again eaten dessert for breakfast when a hot, hearty meal in the dining hall is available to him. Dad doesn't care for the other residents at the retirement community where you and your brother "put me" when your mother died, even though he found the place, bought an apartment there, and efficiently tossed out nearly everything from the house where you grew up (goodbye, all traces of your existence!) without a word to you or your brother.

Using your restrained, superpatient voice, say, "Dad? We can go as soon as you put your seat belt on." Good for you not to use a negative construction like "We can't go until you put your seat belt on," which Dad would take as a criticism. Such turns of phrase invite him to say, "Then we won't go. I don't see why we're going anyway," and likely lead to his getting out of the car and slamming the door. You're already running late, and you'll be lucky to get the doctor, with whom you made this appointment seven months ago, to see him at all.

"Oh, all right," Dad says.

Take deep, cleansing breaths while Dad treats the seat belt like a thing he has never seen, some mystifying contraption invented to thwart him.

First he has to grope around to find the shoulder strap—"Where the hell do they put these things?"—and then he must violently yank and yank at the strap so that it keeps retracting and getting locked in its retracted position. Take more deep breaths as Dad finally yanks it free and then grapples with the strap as if he were in a fight to the death with a furious cobra or a crocodile, like Crocodile Dundee, only frail and flailing and losing.

Painful as it is to witness this struggle, it is not yet time to say, "Dad, let me help you with your seat belt." If you say this now, Dad will say take offense at your treating him "like a three-year-old, for fuck's sake." Dad's language has gotten a lot saltier since your mom died, something you find both amusing and troubling.

Sooner or later, miraculously, the seat belt will release smoothly, long enough for Dad to attempt to buckle it. He does this by stabbing the metal piece on the shoulder strap in the general area of the buckle without looking down. Looking down would be a concession to the capricious despot that is the seat belt. Finally, Dad inserts the metal piece into the buckle. But there's no click.

"Dad? It has to click."

"Jesus fucking Christ!"

Reach over and—gently, calmly—insert the metal piece into the buckle yourself, perhaps even graciously adding, "They're so annoying, right?"

Now, at last, you can begin your journey. You start down the road.

Except that today Dad complains that the shoulder strap "is strangling me" and that he "can't breathe."

"Would you like to sit in the back, in the middle seat? That one doesn't have a shoulder strap, just a belt across your lap," you say.

Surely, you think, he won't take you up on this offer. But Dad is feeling extra-cranky today, and he does. Pull onto the shoulder of the road, help Dad into the backseat, buckle his seat belt for him, and return to driving the car.

"I can't see anything from back here," Dad says.

"Aren't there windows back there too?" you say, because you can't help it.

"I can't see where we're going."

"We're just going a few blocks, to the doctor."

"Not my doctor. Who is this guy, anyway?"

Tell him, for the thousandth time, that this doctor was highly recommended by three of your friends whose parents are experiencing the exact same ailment.

"What kind of doctor is he?" Dad asks.

"He's a gerontologist."

"But that's for old people!"

You've been expecting this. Tell him, lightheartedly, that you are practically old enough to go to a gerontologist yourself.

"Then *you* go to him," says Dad. "How much is this costing, anyway?"

Tell him not to worry; tell him you're paying for it, as you've discussed ad nauseam.

"What's the matter with you people?" Dad says. "No wonder you don't have any money."

You wonder whether by "you people" Dad is referring to you and your brother or to your entire generation. Don't ask, don't ask, don't ask. Do you really want to know? Would that question lead anywhere except to one of those Black Hole conversations with Dad, increasingly contentious and resulting in his demand that you return him home right now?

More cleansing breaths, the way you learned to do in

that meditation class you took. You should have gone to more classes, but you're pretty sure that a million meditation classes wouldn't prepare you for dealing with Dad. Only large doses of drugs would do, and you, alas, have too many responsibilities, like driving Dad to his appointments, to take drugs.

"Why are we even going? There's nothing wrong with me."

Remind Dad that he has fallen five times in as many months.

"Those were accidents." As if this were a different category altogether.

You probably shouldn't say, "I just don't want you to fall and hit your head on the coffee table," but you do, in an effort to make a possible scenario seem more "real."

"I don't have a coffee table."

There's the Black Hole, right there. You didn't see it coming; you never know which words or phrases will be the trigger, the utterance that will turn you both into actors in an absurdist play.

Yes, technically, the low piece of furniture in front of his sofa is not a coffee table; it's a pine chest. But your parents used it as a coffee table in the house where you grew up for, like, thirty years.

Don't get into it. Deep breaths. Good for you.

"I don't know why they call coffee tables *coffee tables* anyway," Dad says. To anyone uninitiated in dealing with Dad, this remark will sound like more contentiousness. But it's not—it's Dad's way of changing the topic. It's his form of a pleasantry.

"That's true," you say. "No one really puts coffee on them, do they? Maybe sometimes, like after dinner, but hardly ever."

"Right! It's stupid!"

"Very stupid! Like *glove compartment*. Who puts gloves in the glove compartment?"

"I did. When I had a car. Which I don't anymore because they took my license away, fucking sons of bitches."

Congratulations. You have arrived at the doctor's office only forty-five minutes late, and the nurse says the doctor will see you shortly. While you wait, tell Dad that after his appointment you'll take him to his favorite diner for coffee and a cheese omelet, your treat.

"You love their omelets," you say. This offer will be greeted as you expect: You spend too much money; your mother made much better omelets; the best coffee is at McDonald's; and he already ate.

You take him anyway. Deep breaths, deep breaths.

WHAT I SAW AT THE MOVIES

I love lists of the top this and the top that, don't you? Top surgeons, top roller coasters, top colleges, top pastrami sandwiches. Someone has done a lot of thinking and decision-making on my behalf, and I'm grateful.

In this spirit, I've come up with the Top Movies of All Time. Maybe you're thinking, Aren't these just *her* choices? Wouldn't someone else make different, equally worthy choices?

No. My choices are the correct choices, and other choices are the wrong choices. My choices are correct because they are made disinterestedly—which, though I have to remind people about this ten times a day, doesn't mean I don't care! *Disinterested* means I'm impartial!—and because I have only listed films with universal themes and appeal, rather than those that I happen to enjoy, which would be self-centered of me.

You're welcome, and here goes:

The Godfather and *The Godfather: Part II* tell the story of Carmela Corleone, a wonderful mother whose son grows up to be a big success. In *Part II*, he builds her a lovely home on the shores of Lake Tahoe right next to his, so she can spend her later years being cared for and paid obeisance to by her offspring, in the comfort every mother so richly deserves. Francesca De Sapio plays the young Carmela, and Morgana King plays the wise matriarch.

The Graduate: In this frisky, high-spirited romp, Mrs. Robinson (Anne Bancroft) is a stylish lady who escapes her loveless marriage to a boorish businessman by finding a randy twenty-one-year-old to seduce. This backfires eventually, but not before she has gotten a summer's worth of terrific sex out of it.

Chinatown: Ida Sessions (Diane Ladd) is every Hollywood starlet's nightmare—a fortysomething actress who's scrambling for any part she can get. To make ends meet, Ida takes a sketchy "acting" job impersonating the wealthy Evelyn Mulwray, part of a scheme cooked up by the real Mrs. Mulwray's degenerate husband. The gig has trouble written all over it, but what else is Ida to do? Women everywhere will identify with Ida's plight—a woman in her prime, whose talents go unrewarded, to say the least.

The Wizard of Oz: Careworn Auntie Em (Clara Blandick) leads a hardscrabble life on a broken-down Kansas farm straight out of a Walker Evans photograph. Of no help at all to her is the niece she has generously taken in, a dreamy, self-involved girl who moons around wishing she were elsewhere. When her impulse-control issues get the better of her, the girl runs away, leaving Auntie Em to deal with the girl's disappearance as well as a nasty tornado.

Shane: This 1953 classic tells the tale of Marian Starrett and her lone campaign to end gun violence in the Old West. The whole town is gun crazy, including her husband and son, and things don't exactly improve with the arrival of a handsome professional gunslinger. All the males develop big man crushes on him, which get more intense the closer he gets to a shoot-out with another gunslinger. Marian's pacifism can't hold a candle to all this phallic energy, but she just keeps at it, bless her heart. Jean Arthur plays the lovely, quixotic heroine.

The Departed: Vera Farmiga stars in this 2006 Martin Scorsese film as a brilliant Boston therapist who learns a hard but important lesson: It's a very bad idea to date one of your patients, and an even worse one to date two.

Sophie's Choice: Yetta Zimmerman runs a boardinghouse in Brooklyn just after World War II. It's a lot of work, especially when two of her boarders turn out to be a complete lunatic and his codependent

Polish girlfriend. He bullies and yells at the girlfriend, pounds on the piano at all hours, and keeps loudly moving out in the middle of the night, only to return the next day. Any other landlady would kick them both out, but Yetta, played beautifully by Rita Karin, remains amazingly patient and compassionate, even mourning the couple's untimely end.

Lincoln is all about Mary Todd Lincoln, played with depth and poignancy by Sally Field. Don't you just love Sally Field? How she hangs in there, doing fine work decade after decade while Meryl Streep gets all the best parts? And hats off to Field for fighting for the role after director Steven Spielberg told her she was too old looking to play the forty-two-year-old first lady. "Daniel [Day-Lewis] will look old and worn and thin and I will look old and worn and fat, and that's what they were," she told Spielberg. Way to go, sister!

Les Misérables is a hilarious look at the life of a slatternly but clever middle-aged innkeeper. Played by a delightful Helena Bonham Carter, the character manages to get through the lean post–French Revolution years by making some savvy financial deals. Sequel, please!

Silver Linings Playbook is about a kindhearted, overworked housewife whose husband and grown child are both insane and eat her out of house and home. Jacki Weaver plays the leading role with forbearance and endless good humor.

Finally, what list of great films would be complete without a shout-out to the beloved *Mary Poppins*? Glynis Johns stars as Mrs. Banks, the dynamic suffragette who discovers how much she can accomplish in the world once she hires a babysitter.

WHAT I'VE LEARNED

Just when you think you're on terra firma, whoa, there you go, sucked down into some awful hellhole. A snowstorm blows the huge tree in your yard onto your house, turning your front porch into kindling, but the "wind deductible" in your insurance policy is $30,000 and it costs $29,998.45 to fix the porch. That lovely nightgown in a gift box shoved under some papers in your husband's study was not, it turns out, purchased with you in mind. What can you do about it? Nothing, usually. Not a thing.

Thank goodness for popular entertainment, where threats are well-known and crystal clear, and there is always a way out. What a comfort! That's why I like to soothe myself to sleep by reviewing everything I've learned from television and movies. The older I get, the more I realize that their lessons are the only things I know to be true:

I am certainly not going *back into the house* where something bad or creepy has happened to me already.

I am never going to a *carnival* or a *fair*, particularly if there is *happy calliope music* playing. Apropos of fairs, there is no way I am attending the Feast of San Gennaro under any circumstances. Someone will get shot, and I don't want to be in the way.

You will not find me owning, or spending any time with, a *ventriloquist's dummy*, or the kind of *doll that "walks" and "talks."*

If I become an astronaut, am I leaving the spaceship under any circumstances? No, I am not—not to fix anything on the outside of the spaceship while tethered to the ship by one *not-that-strong cord*; not to explore the terrain of the planet we land on, a dusty place that looks like it has *no life-forms* but surely will, ones that *do not wish me well.*

If I get arrested for something, in no way am I accepting the arresting detectives' invitation to *"just go down to the station"* with them to *"have a chat."* Everybody knows what happens when you go down to the station to have a chat—they put you in "the box" and grill you for hours, and before you know it, you have confessed to some horrible crime you didn't even commit—and yet so many people, people who should know better, go anyway. Not I. If they want to have a chat, we will go directly to *my lawyer's office*, with my lawyer doing all the talking.

If I forget my no-going-down-to-the-station rule and find myself in the box being brutally interrogated by the police, I will certainly not be dumb enough to *accept re-freshments*, particularly a *can of soda*. How many times do we have to learn that a can of soda is a transparent effort to get DNA from our saliva?

Conversely, if I become a detective, here is one police-work rule I am never forgetting: *backup, backup, backup.* What is the point of all that training if I don't use backup the only time I need it?

Okay, sure, I know my partner is indisposed—sometimes it's a "good" reason, like he's just been shot in the leg by the bad guy and is therefore incapable of keeping up with me while we give chase through streets and across rooftops and down alleyways—but *that's not a good enough reason.* I will gladly lose the bad guy before I continue without backup. Going in without backup is for sure going to get me shot, or hanging from a roof ledge while the bad guy stomps on my fingers. A big NO to that. I will just talk to the captain and get a *substitute partner* for the day. That's all there is to it.

If someone *poisons my dog* or other pet and *leaves its corpse* on my front porch, I will not mistake this for an isolated, freak event, but know that it is merely the beginning of a cascade of *progressively more terrible* events.

I am never going to go into a *parking garage* at night. Correction: I am never going to go into a parking garage, period. Ditto any apartment building's *basement laundry room*—op. cit., not going.

If I find that *pieces of furniture* have relocated themselves around my house, I will not "gaslight" myself by thinking, Oh, maybe I forgot I moved them, when it is all too obvious that they have been moved by *paranormal activity*.

I am never going into a *raffish bar*, especially not one with a name like *O'Malley's* or *O'anything's*. Nothing good will happen to me in there, and whatever does happen will probably happen in the disgusting ladies' room.

If I am reckless and go in anyway and the worst happens to me (i.e., I am killed by Westies or another gang), I will know that the guys who did it will get the priest who molested them as children, who has to do everything they say so they won't kill him, to hide my corpse under the parish house, depriving my loved ones of the small comfort of at least *having a body to bury*.

In terms of other bars, I am never going into a cocktail lounge with a *giant fish tank* at the bar. I will end up falling into it somehow, and having to swim around in my clothes, surprising and amusing the patrons at the bar but disgracing and humiliating myself.

I am never going to trust any contemporary artist, or anyone in the *downtown art scene*. They are snooty and always think they're so great, which makes them think they can get away with anything, including murdering people. If there is a murder, everyone knows that the artist or la-di-da gallery owner did it, and I do not want the murdered person to be me.

I will steer clear of all *teenagers*. Because if the art gallery owner didn't do it, the teenagers did. Particularly if they are rich and entitled and wear the uniform—the navy-blue blazer with the school crest and gray slacks, or pleated plaid skirt—of the tony private day school they attend. It doesn't matter how politely they shake hands; you never know when they've woven you into their warped web of resentments. If I'm dating their widower father, they figure I'm after their inheritance, and that's the end of me— poisoned with some tasteless yet toxic brew they've cooked up in the chem lab at St. Switherington's and stirred into my iced tea, or pushed quietly down the stairs while I visit their weekend estate in the Hamptons, breaking my neck and dooming me to live the rest of my life as a quadriplegic.

Speaking of resentments, and of being rich, if I do become rich, I am definitely treating all of my servants with the proper respect, thus quelling any desire to murder me. These include the obvious staff members—my maid, my trainer, my chef, my driver, et al.—but I am going to be extra-careful not to forget the helpers who work less frequently, who would be easy for me to overlook: the quiet Mexican guy who comes to weed, the tuner of my Steinway grand piano, the strange fellow who biannually winds the priceless grandfather clock in my vast foyer. "Good morning, Mr. So-and-So," I will say in greeting them. "Here's three hundred dollars, as a thank-you just for coming. And bill me whatever you wish!"

As for my health, I am never sitting or standing next to anyone who is *coughing innocently*. There are no innocent coughs, only ones that signal *imminent pandemics*. I am going to be particularly wary of getting anywhere near *coughing children*, as their cute looks will make me think, wrongly, that they could not possibly be incubating a new kind of plague.

In regard to allowing people to wire me to machines that will implant ideas in my subconscious by *manipulating my dreams*: Will I agree to this? No, thank you, I will not. I know that the result will be my inability to tell the difference between my dreams and my real life, and I have enough trouble with this already. Exception: if the idea that is being implanted has me diving into a *giant chocolate cake* or *having intimate relations with George Clooney*, I will do this.

I think you may at this point be able to guess my position on *camping in the woods* with friends. Camping in the woods with friends would be like my sending out an engraved invitation: "Come and get me, crazy people. I'm just here in front of the campfire, listening to my friends tell scary stories about crazy people in the woods, and laughing off the stories, so that when you do get me, it will almost serve me right." No, no, sir, *nyet*. No camping. Not going. Some things you just know are true.

SALT AND PEPPER

For a while, what I missed most in turning from a married person to a single person was the act that we were as a couple. I don't mean an act as in a piece of fakery, although toward the end it was kind of fake.

I mean it in the sense of how we were out in the world. We made a good couple, I think. We were entertaining. We held up our end of things. I had a joke I'd tell about a priest and a speeding ticket—I won't tell it here because it won't sound funny, and anyway I can't remember the punch line, but it was funny. I told a lot of stories about my misadventures, like the time I sat down on a freshly painted park bench and then had to walk down Fifth Avenue with green stripes all over the back of my dress.

My husband was more of a gadfly. He did a great riff on why *Death of a Salesman* isn't a good play. I didn't agree with him—I think *Death of a Salesman* is a heartwrenching play—but it was fun to hear him carry on

about it, like listening to someone poke fun of Mother
Teresa.

We got sick of each other's routines, but that came much
later. For many years, we each thought the other was a hoot.
And we complemented each other: I'd ask people about their
children; he'd talk about the next election.

You spend twenty-five years going out into the world
together—dinner parties, work-related parties, weddings,
visits with relatives—and how you are together becomes not
so much an act as part of your identity. You're half of a
matched set, like a pair of salt and pepper shakers. This
isn't just how other people see you—it's how you see yourself. It feels safe. You always know who your plus-one is
going to be. You always have someone to stand next to at
one of those cocktail parties where you don't know a soul.

Then, suddenly, the other half of the set isn't there, and it
just feels . . . weird, like you forgot to do something important
before you left the house—to put on lipstick, or your coat.

For the first time, you have tender feelings for Jerry Lewis,
for how much he must have dreaded being up there onstage
all alone, post-Dino. Maybe you won't be enough of an act.
Maybe you were never that amusing. Maybe there will be
some horrible gaping hole in the conversation where he
used to talk. Maybe someone will ask you about the situation in Chechnya and you'll have to say, "I'm sorry, my ex-
husband was much better on former Soviet republics."

Or maybe people will worry that you have some new,
awful act—that you're bitter or furious or a nervous wreck
about your single circumstances and that you'll launch into

some endless tirade—and will steer clear of you, dreading
that you'll try your new act out on them. Maybe you'll be
subtly but unmistakably shunned, just because you make
people uncomfortable—they haven't seen you since you were
married, and they don't know what to say.

Not since the seventh grade have you had such social
anxiety. It feels bad, and humiliating, more humiliating
because you can't believe you're such a wimp (although at
first people do talk about you, which you can tell because
there's a moment, just like in the movies, when you enter a
room and other people in it suddenly fall silent).

And you know what? All the worry is a big fat waste of
time. You make yourself go out and see people, and it turns
out you're enough of an act. You make people laugh. They
make you laugh. There's more than enough for you to talk
about and to ask them about.

You walk into rooms full of strangers, and it's only scary
for about ten minutes. Yes, people do feel sorry for you for
a while, but the way they show it isn't to avoid you but to
ask you to do things. They invite you to the movies or out for
coffee or over for dinner. They take care of you. Sometimes
this makes you feel so grateful that you shed a tear when
you think about it. Then, when some time has gone by—
less time than you think, I promise—you ask them back.
You have a dinner party, then another, and the men who
come—your girlfriends' husbands, your men friends—help
you do things without being asked: bartending, carving the

leg of lamb, moving extra chairs to the table, things they think your husband may have helped you with in the past, even though he didn't.

And you all have a fine, rollicking time, and you think, I can do this.

ROGER AILES'S NEW, ENLIGHTENED CODE OF SEXUAL CONDUCT

This just in:

Roger Ailes, the disgraced former chairman and CEO of Fox News, has completed a week at an intensive "Yes Means Yes" seminar on sexual conduct. The seminar, which Mr. Ailes attended on the advice of his attorneys, instructs participants on the new "affirmative consent" standards now mandated at many colleges and universities: Those initiating sexual activity must receive a clear verbal "Yes," or a positive nonverbal equivalent, to engage in a sexual encounter, every step of the way.

Mr. Ailes reports that he is "a changed man" following the seminar, admitting that he is "just an old guy who didn't know any better." To prove his good faith, Mr. Ailes has written the following "code of conduct" for himself:

When a female employee, or potential employee, enters my office, and I greet her by locking the door and telling her to lift her skirt so that I may see her underpants, or to bend over so that I may "get a good look" at her buttocks, I will try to remember that her silence, or "I don't think so," may not be an attempt to get me to persuade her with flattering references to her smoking bod.

When I then propose that she have sex with me, and with my friends, in exchange for a job, promotion, or raise, using my signature phrase "If you want to play with the big boys, you have to lay with the big boys," I will understand that a response such as "That's illegal, and I'm going to report you," while ambiguous, signifies that I should pursue another topic, like showing her the issue of *Maxim* that I keep on my office coffee table and telling her to take off all of her clothes, lie on my sofa, and strike the hot poses featured in the magazine.

If she declines, I will not interpret her response to mean "Sure, but let's get hammered first." I will proceed accordingly, to wit: chasing her about my office while shouting, "Come to Poppy!" Once I have cornered her, I will grab her breasts and fondle them.

I understand that a response such as punching me in my face, saying, "Get away from me, you revolting pig," and/or fleeing my office fall short of a "Yes" to my overtures, however gracefully I have executed them.

If she flees my office and runs, say, into the ladies' room, barricading the door with her body, I will respect the clear boundary she has set and wait patiently outside the ladies' room until she believes that I have left the area. When she emerges, I will present my genitals, which I have taken out of my trousers, and demand that she kiss them.

If she declines, I will understand that she is "uptight" about performing this activity in an office setting. Accordingly, I will place my genitals back inside my trousers, zip up my fly, and invite her to join me for dinner and a blow job.

In the event that she fails to reply with a "Yes," I will conclude that fine dining isn't her "thing" and instead invite her to cruise around Manhattan with me on a private yacht while giving me blow jobs.

If I do not receive affirmative consent for this, my final offer, I will not employ punitive actions such as shunning her, docking her pay, transferring her to Tijuana, or ruining her professional reputation.

On the contrary, I will urge her to sue me. Win or lose, I will collect forty million dollars in severance, find a new job in no time, and set about advancing the careers of a whole new group of young women. It's really what I'm best at.

FALLING

One moment I'm walking along Forty-Second Street, and the next moment—a chip in the sidewalk that catches the heel (Thick, sensible heels! They're Aerosoles!) of my shoe? A slick of some Tennessee visitor's spat-out chewing tobacco?— I'm falling, falling, taking a face-forward flier, right in front of Port Authority. Oh, man, that sidewalk is going to be so cruel.

Not that many years ago, my prayer as I hurtled through space would have been "Please don't let anyone I know see me when I land, all splayed out on the sidewalk, and think I fell because I'm drunk and then tell people I know that they saw me fall down drunk." That's still my first thought when I see someone fall down on the street, especially if it's a street with a lot of crummy bars on it, or here at Port Authority, where, no matter how much they clean up the interior, it is still Vagrant Central outside, with that accompanying miasma, that *eau de* Port Authority, of marijuana and Old Grand-Dad and puke.

But now that worry seems so callow, so full of jejune self-consciousness. Now my prayers are without vanity, and desperate: Please, if I break some bone or snap some tendon, will one of the people who is watching me fall be charitable enough to help me after I land? And when I break the bones I am about to break, let them not be both wrists but only one, preferably my right wrist, as I am left-handed and could still type with that one hand if I had to? Also, if possible, let the bone(s) I break not be my pelvic bone, as I hear that's particularly painful, and I just don't have the time, or a steady enough income, for the six months of recovery?

I haven't injured myself yet, but even writing these words feels like I'm wildly tempting fate, setting myself up for some spectacular crippling spill. Three of my friends were taken down by black ice on Manhattan sidewalks last winter (broken wrist, broken wrist, broken leg). I myself did a full belly flop onto Fifty-Sixth Street after slipping on an evil slick of black ice, my take-out coffee from the McDonald's at Fifty-Sixth and Eighth spraying into the air. In shock, I stood up and took myself and my coffee cup back into McDonald's, where I asked the young woman behind the counter if she would consider refilling it for free due to my little accident, and to my delight, she did.

While she filled it, a woman in a traffic-cop uniform who was standing nearby, drinking her coffee and listening, looked at me with concern and shook her head. I remembered that I'd seen her at that very intersection, at Fifty-Sixth and Eighth, the day before. "You're the third person who fell on that ice this morning," she said. "I'm gonna get them to put some salt on that." Not until I got home did I take a good look at myself: my coat covered in grit, my tights torn at the knee, my knees bloodied. I looked like I'd survived a bomb blast.

Nevertheless, I walked away from the incident thinking, How sweet of the girl behind the counter to give me that coffee. How good of the traffic cop to get whoever puts salt on sidewalks to do that. Who says New Yorkers are cold and unfeeling? An hour after that, I took this anecdote with me to the municipal courthouse downtown. My husband was suing me for divorce and had decided to take me to trial, an endeavor that had cost us both tens of thousands of dollars. Now, incredibly, here we were, the day before the trial, at court, if you could call it that—a big room with grimy windows and sloppy stacks of boxes filled with papers. Our judge, whose office the room appeared to be, nodded off behind his desk, while our lawyers were in the men's room bickering and trying to agree on a settlement that would keep the trial from commencing, an event none of them wanted, a trial being a total crapshoot for both sides.

Anyway, I told them the story (I know, you're wondering why I was chatting them up at all; the truth was that I still didn't think, even at this eleventh hour, that my husband would actually go through with a trial, which was going to cost us even more money than we'd already hemorrhaged. Only people with millions of dollars or custody issues to fight over have reason enough to go to trial, and we had neither): how the ice slick was so bad that three people had fallen on it; how conscientious and thoughtful the traffic cop was to arrange for salt to fix that nasty patch of ice.

My husband listened impassively to the whole story, then he smiled, a smile I had come to recognize as his "what assholes these mortals be" smile.

"Three people fall," he said, "and *then* she gets the idea."

This had not occurred to me. Right then, I knew two things:

1. Our responses, so different, said everything there was to say about our relationship; and, on a related note,
2. Of course we would be going to trial. Any fool knew that. Except, perhaps, the kind of fool who thought it was "nice" for a traffic cop to wait until three people nearly broke their backs before she decided to correct the situation.

But I digress.

My turn is so coming. Because now my body is going—bones more brittle, tendons thinning, cartilage wearing out. I never knew exactly what tendons and cartilage were before, but I do now, because my friends keep doing dreadful things to theirs and I've had to google them to understand their injuries.

And the bones! Who knew there were so many different bones in the human body! I'd always thought there were about twelve, and you could sing them all in that ditty about the leg bone being connected to the thighbone, and so on. Apparently, the human foot alone has more bones than a flounder, and my friends have broken every one of them; I could teach a foot-anatomy class from the names of all the bones I know now.

Friends slip missing the last step of their stairway or getting out of bed—or just doing nothing! Just standing in their driveway!—and there goes their third metatarsal or their proximal phalanx. The surgeon fills them full of plates and rods and screws, and more pins than a voodoo doll, and they have to wear a huge plastic boot for many weeks, and when the surgeon examines them after all those weeks, it still hasn't healed properly, and they need three more surgeries to correct it. Even after all that, it doesn't feel right for many months, during which time they shuffle along as slowly and gingerly as ninety-seven-year-olds to avoid the shooting stab of pain that comes when they apply any pressure to the tiny, sort-of-repaired bone.

Then they have to wear running shoes, or some kind of special orthopedic shoe, all the time, even with dresses. Please don't let me fracture something that means I will have to wear running shoes with dresses. If I do, it'll be my karmic punishment for thirty years of silently mocking the women in my apartment building who went to work dressed this way.

There are all the other bones to break besides the foot ones. I'd thought hip breaking was the province of very old ladies, but my friend Polly—lithe! limber! not yet sixty!—had to get a whole new hip after taking a spill and landing on hers. And don't even think *rotator cuff*. If you think it, you will rend it.

Please let whoever comes over to help me not be a group

of jolly, overly helpful young backpackers from Australia who will say "No worries!" and insist on lifting me, and in doing so jostle the disk I ruptured in my fall and leave me paralyzed from the waist down. Please let it just be a Port Authority bum, who will kindly fish my cell phone out of my purse so I can call 911 and then wander off, though not before stealing the cash in my wallet. That would be fine.

What hospital am I going to be taken to? When the ambulance comes, do I get a say in this? Can I say, "Could you please take me to the Hospital for Special Surgery, where they specialize in orthopedics," or is that considered too uppity?

When they take me wherever they are going to take me, please don't let me get some child surgeon, some resident who has been on duty for eighty-three hours and gets my elbow, or whatever I have splintered, confused with my big toe.

After I break whatever it is I am going to break and am recovering from whatever surgeries I will require, please don't let me get addicted to pain pills. I don't want to have to go to East New York and buy OxyContin on a street corner. I'm too old for that. I won't be able to tell the drug pushers from the tattooed youngsters from Scarsdale who have come to the city to buy their drugs for the weekend. It will take me all day to find a real pusher, many hours of hobbling around on my healing though horribly painful sundered tibia, and when I finally find the pusher, he'll probably be an undercover cop, and I'll have to go to jail. And then go through withdrawal huddled in a corner of my cell, shivering and sweating, mocked and hooted at by my cellmates.

I am going to injure myself, that is a certainty, but please don't let me suffer the kind of injury that will require me to go to rehab to learn how to walk again. People I know keep breaking and shredding things and the next minute they're in rehab, somewhere in White Plains, or Rockland County.

They're there for weeks, and if you offer to visit them, they say, "No, no, don't come, it's too awful here," and when they return, they won't even talk about it. You say, "Were the physical therapists nice?" And they say, "Not really. I don't want to talk about it." "Well, how was the food at least?" "I don't know. I didn't eat it."

It's like the whole experience has shamed them in some way. Or like they saw a ghost, and it was them. Please, please don't let me have to go to rehab.

I have a dream, a new dream of my advancing years. Wouldn't it be great to have one of those metal walkers to walk around with, just to prevent injury? If you felt yourself starting to go down, you'd just grip it and steady yourself. That would be great. Pathetic, but great.

Today, here in front of Port Authority, baby Jesus, or whoever, has decided to perform another miracle and spare me. My wrists break my fall and stay intact. My palms are scraped raw from the sidewalk, and a few little pebbles are embedded in them, but I walk away to fall another day.

PLEASE DON'T INVITE ME

Are you having a party? Can I come? I love parties, even parties that other people might not think sound like much fun: office retirement parties, friends' toddler's nursery school graduations, bar and bat mitzvah parties, book parties, dogs' birthday parties, brises. Well, not the bris itself, but the brunch after the bris. I like seeing people, and usually there's cake, and I love cake. Even commercial sheet cake, with that icing that has no flavor except sugar. I used to pooh-pooh sheet cake, but now I like it, for some reason. I always ask for a corner piece so I can get more icing.

I also like other gatherings and events, so please invite me to those too. If I'm in town, I'll come. I like seders, readings of your new play, school fairs, and benefits, although if you are inviting me to one of those benefits with expensive tickets, you will have to pay for my seat at your table. Thank you so much for doing that.

Some events, however, I just cannot do. I don't want to

get anyone's nose out of joint, so I thought I would offer them here, prophylactically, in case you are planning to invite me to one of them. Not to be rude, but so you can invite someone else who will enjoy it and be a better guest.

Thank you for not inviting me to a professional basketball game, even if your tickets are for the really good seats where the movie stars sit. In fact, please don't invite me to any sports game. I wish I could see what other people see in watching sports—the human body at its most templelike, the balletic beauty of teamwork, the thrill of competition. That metaphysical, practically mystical experience people seem to have while watching baseball. Whatever the game may be, I just cannot keep my mind on it. After the first five minutes or so, my mind wanders and wanders. Where's the hot-dog guy? Hunh, here's a cloud in the shape of George Washington's head. I went to Mount Vernon once. No, that was Monticello.

Also, I always end up cheering for both teams, so the losing one won't feel bad. You wouldn't want me there anyway.

Forgive me for sounding coldhearted, but please don't invite me to a two-hour funeral or memorial service. Two hours is too long, no matter how accomplished and fabulous the dead person was. Also, please don't invite me to a service where all of the eulogists are famous. Famous eulogists talk about themselves rather than the dead person, and one per funeral is more than enough. Also, they usually didn't know the dead person that well, so they just tell some old story about the supposedly hilarious thing the dead person said while holding forth drunkenly at Elaine's in 1973 while his spouse and children, no doubt, waited for him to come home for dinner.

Please don't invite me to one of those art openings where there is no food whatsoever except a small bowl of salted peanuts at the bar. That's just rude.

Speaking of not getting enough to eat, please don't invite me to dinner at a macrobiotic restaurant. I wish I liked this sort of food, but I just can't. I feel like I'm being punished for something I didn't do. Although once I had the best German chocolate cake I have ever tasted at a raw food restaurant in San Francisco. Sometimes I think about calling the restaurant and asking how they made it taste so delicious without using butter or sugar or eggs or flour or German chocolate, but I'm not sure I want to know.

Thank you for not inviting me to any event that would involve my driving in the state of New Jersey. I like New Jersey; it's the impenetrable highway "system" that I hate. As far as I'm concerned, the Pulaski Skyway is the portal to hell. I have wept, lost, on roadsides all over New Jersey. Even with a GPS, I will get to your event two hours late and in a terrible mood, as if you yourself had invented the tangled strands of spaghetti that are the roads of your state.

Is it just me, or is Fashion Week every other week now? In any case, thank you for thinking of me, but please don't invite me. I just don't care about Fashion Week. I don't care, I don't care, I don't care. Also, it bothers me that people you would never think would go to Fashion Week show up there. I once saw a photo of Lou Reed, may he rest in peace, at

Fashion Week. Brilliant Lou Reed! Why was he at Fashion Week when he could have been at home with his wife, the pixie genius Laurie Anderson?

I also don't want to know about my future, so please don't invite me to any gathering where you think it would be fun to have a fortune-teller, astrologer, or tarot-card or tea-leaf reader tell my fortune. Particularly if they are good at what they do. I just don't want to know. Too many things have happened to me already. Unless my fortune is "Congratulations, the rest of your life will be uneventful," I would rather be in the dark.

Please don't invite me to a movie that I think will include a car chase but is actually just one long car chase. I love some chasing in a movie, but it has to come in between the parts where the characters talk to each other, so I can care about why they are being chased or are chasing. To me, the wonderful *Catch Me If You Can* is the perfect example of this kind of movie, so please invite me to a movie like that.

To finish up: Please don't invite me to rock climb, even a modest peak or boulder, even a fake one with ledges designed for easy gripping; to the opera (I'm sorry, I know it's my loss); or to watch you do your stand-up comedy routine on the night you have decided not to do your act but to read something from your memoir-writing class instead. I like magic shows, though, and bingo nights, and bowling parties, and I hardly ever get asked to those, so please count me in. I would particularly love to be invited to do that kind of bowling you do in the dark, with glow-in-the-dark bowling balls. It sounds like everyone could be equally bad at it, which would be right up my alley (alley! ha!) and would involve a lot of potato chips and other delicious salty snack foods. And nothing says fun like those crazy bowling shoes, which crack me up. So invite me. I am so there.

ACKNOWLEDGMENTS

I would like to offer my heartfelt thanks to Sarah Crichton, splendid, patient editor, who had the idea for this book; dream agent Steve Ross; and *New Yorker* editors Susan Morrison and Emma Allen. I am grateful beyond words to a wide circle of friends and family: you sustain me, every day. A traveler's abundant thanks to Polly Draper and Michael Wolff, Nina Bang-Jensen and Jeffrey Kampelman, Naomi Hample, Gaylen Moore, Marisa Smith, Barbara and Rob Wallner, and Lucy Mitchell and Rez Williams, who have hosted me endlessly. Gratitude as well to Liz Allen and Cindy Allen, the mighty women who hold a sprawling clan together; and to the skilled men, Carter Hakala, Chuck Lewis, and Jim Sharp among them, whose labors hold my house together.

The following pieces, or versions of them, appeared in various publications. "I'm Awake," "My Gathas," "Can I Borrow That?," "My Gratitudes," "My New Feminist Cop Show," "I Have to Go Now," "The Trouble with Nature,"

"Speak, Memory," "What I've Learned," and "Roger Ailes's New, Enlightened Code of Sexual Conduct" appeared in *The New Yorker*, either in print or online. "I'm Awake" also appeared in *The 50 Funniest American Writers*: An Anthology of Humor from Mark Twain to* The Onion *(*According to Andy Borowitz)* (Library of America, 2011) and *Disquiet, Please!: More Humor Writing from* The New Yorker (Random House, 2008). "Swagland" appeared in *Vogue*. "It's About Time," "Hair Today, Gone Tomorrow," "What I Saw at the Movies," "Salt and Pepper," and "Please Don't Invite Me" appeared in *More* magazine. "Hair Today, Gone Tomorrow" also appeared in *The Moth*, an anthology of stories told at the Moth. "I Can't Get That Penis out of My Mind" appeared in *The Huffington Post*. "L.L.Bean and Me" appeared in *TSR: The Southampton Review*, vol. II, no. 1, and a portion of the essay was also included in *I Got Sick Then I Got Better* (Dramatists Play Service, 2013). "Dream On, You Motherfucking Mother" appeared in *Kugelmass* magazine. "Seconds" appeared in *Feed Me!: Writers Dish About Food, Eating, Weight, and Body Image* (Ballantine Books, 2009).